C000184268

The
Mailva
Handbook

British Bus Publishing

The Mailvan Handbook

The Royal Mail Group currently operates a fleet of about 33,000 commercial vehicles, making it one of the largest commercial fleet operations in the U.K. What makes the Royal Mail unusual is the diversity of types in its fleet, ranging from mopeds and small vans to 38-tonne artics and trailers, and including passenger-carrying vehicles such as cars, crewbuses and postbuses and a few full-sized buses and coaches.

Royal Mail has its origins in the General Post Office with a formal postal system established by Act of Parliament in 1657. Motorised mail transport, initially provided by private contractors, began in 1897 at the same time as the introduction of a daily delivery of letters to every household. The first use by the GPO of its own motorised transport was in 1914, when twenty motor cycle combinations were bought with wicker or metal side-carriers of 18 cubic feet (cf) capacity. Difficulties with contractors after the First World War led to trials with two former War Department Fords and this was followed by the purchase of the first new mailvans in 1920. The use of GPO mailvans expanded considerably during the 1920s and 1930s, initially using Ford vans and BSA motor cycle combinations and later Morris or Morris-Commercial vans, often at the expense of contractors whose services were no longer required.

In October 1969, the GPO became the Post Office Corporation and in 1981, the telephone service, Post Office Telephones was demerged to form

British Telecommunications. In 1986, the Post Office reorganised as three separate business units – Royal Mail Letters, Royal Mail Parcels and Post Office Counters. Subsequently the Parcels business adopted the title Parcelforce, later Parcelforce Worldwide. More recently, the Post Office became a plc, Consignia plc, in March 2001 following Royal Assent of the Postal Service Act, but the brand names, Royal Mail, Parcelforce Worldwide and the Post Office were retained for the three businesses set up in 1986. Consignia was almost universally disliked and the name changed to the Royal Mail Group in November 2002.

This Handbook illustrates the principal types of vehicle used on mail duties by the Post Office and its successors over the past twenty-five years. Each vehicle carries a fleet number known as the serial number with the current system introduced in 1971. Each serial number is made up of seven figures, the first represents the final digit of the financial year of purchase, the next two figures relate to the type code of the size or type of vehicle and the final four numbers are the individual vehicle numbers.

This type code has been used as the basis of this Handbook. In the original 1971 system, the type codes were allocated roughly in size order for mailvans, then tractors and trailers, and then the more specialised vehicles. More information on mailvans can be obtained in other publications of the Post Office Vehicle Club. It can be contacted at 32 Russell Way, Leighton Buzzard, LU7 3NG or via its website www.povehclub.org.uk.

Front cover: When the Ford Escort went out of production in 2002, Royal Mail's choice as its small van was the latest design of Vauxhall Combo with a five year contract for up to 20,000 vans placed in November 2002. Over fifteen thousand vans have been delivered to date and it seems likely that during 2006 virtually all the Royal Mail's fleet of small mail vans will be based on this single model, the first time that this has occurred since the Ford Anglia was introduced into the Royal Mail fleet in April 1964, breaking the monopoly of the Morris Minor. EX05XTH (with serial number 4024860), new in March 2005, it was photographed parked in the Kirkbymoorside town centre in North Yorkshire, where it is based, in July 2005. *D Longbottom*

Fronticepiece: Daewoo Avia announced in May 2005 that it had secured a contract from Royal Mail to supply Avia D75 chassis-cabs for five years. The initial batch comprised of twenty-five mailvans fitted with 740cf (cubic feet) bodywork by Derek Jones Bodywork Ltd of Kettering, another new manufacturer for Royal Mail. The order was completed in early October and this view shows the first of batch, MX55TXD (5610730). The vehicles are expected to be concentrated in the Leeds and Sheffield areas. *Royal Mail Vehicle Services*

Opposite: Royal Mail in Scotland in 2001 identified two rural delivery walks that it wished to motorise using quadbikes, at Kerrera and Knoydart. Further details of this vehicle are on page 4. In its place, a standard Ford Escort van was supplied and this was subsequently replaced by a standard Vauxhall Combo mailvan in November 2004. Quadbike Y847KNE (0000001) is pictured at Fort William in August 2003 – it was auctioned two months later with just 356 miles to its credit in Royal Mail service. No front registration plate is required as the 49cc petrol-engined machine is licensed as a motorcycle. *C M Hogan*

ISBN 1 904875 03 3   © British Bus Publishing Ltd, December 2005
Published by *British Bus Publishing Ltd*, 16 St Margaret's Drive, Telford, TF1 3PH
Telephone: 01952 255669 - Facsimile: 01952 222397 - www.britishbuspublishing.co.uk

Types 00 and 01

Type code 00 was allocated in 1971 to Raleigh mopeds used on mail delivery work, mainly in rural areas. These were first introduced in 1962 and were bought in quantity from 1967 to 1970, thereafter being superseded by the Puch MV50 moped. Mopeds used for telegram delivery carried the separate code 66.

The subsequent use of code 00 has been limited to a batch of fifty Ford Fiesta petrol-engined mailcars bought in 1983 (3000001-50) and more recently to a single Piaggio Ape 50 3-wheel mailvan fitted with a 49cc petrol engine (0000001) bought in 2000 for use at Knoydart, a peninsula accessed by boat from Mallaig to motorise a rural delivery walk. The original intention had been to purchase a second quadbike (see type code 67) for this duty but licensing regulations prevented a quadbike being registered as other than as an agricultural vehicle. Unfortunately, it proved unsuitable for use at Knoydart, mainly because of the central front wheel, and after little use, it was declared unsuitable and it was auctioned in October 2003.

The Vauxhall Astramax was bought by Royal Mail in the three years from 1991 to 1993, as an alternative to the Ford Escorts whose reliability was giving Royal Mail some concern following the change from mark IV to mark V versions. Vauxhall Astramax 90cf J986VSG (1011588) was photographed outside Culross Post Office in July 1993. Being a Scottish vehicle, it carries the King's cypher, rather than the Queen's cypher used in England, Wales and Northern Ireland. *M D Street*

Parcelforce had a requirement for small vans and bought both Fords and Vauxhalls. Ford Escort 80cf H248HNC (0015047) photographed in January 1995 at Stretford, Manchester, shows the early Parcelforce livery complete with Royal Mail lettering and cypher. Ford Escort vans bought for Royal Mail duties were coded 87 rather than 01. *P Eckersley*

Type code 01 was allocated in 1971 to the batch of fifty Reliant Supervan 3-wheelers bought in 1970. The next use of the code was on the Bedford HA mailvan, derived from the Vauxhall Viva car, bought for use as a mailvan between 1975 and 1978.

The code was then used for a number of experimental mailvans in the 1988-1990 period with two Peugeot 309 mailvans (8010001/2) in 1988, a Renault Extra (9010001), two Citroën C15Ds (9010002/3) in 1989 and a further Citroën C15D (0010001) in 1990.

Royal Mail turned to the Vauxhall Astramax 365 1.7D in 1991 after it expressed dissatisfaction with the Mark V version of the Ford Escort introduced the previous year. Vauxhall Astramaxes were obtained for three years, with 1,814 bought in 1991, 2,567 in 1992 and 2,500 in 1993.

Meanwhile Parcelforce had found a use for small vans at its depots and adopted code 01 for these vans, buying twelve Astramaxes with Bedford badging in 1989 (9015001-12), two more with Vauxhall badging (0015001/2) and forty-six Ford Escort diesel vans (0015003-48) in 1990, eighty-one more Vauxhall Astramax 365s in 1992, sixty-two Ford Escort 55s in 1994, twenty-one more Ford Escorts in 1996 and in 1997, a mixture of Ford Escorts (7015001-84) and Vauxhall Combo 1.7D vans (7015085-99). Use of type code 01 for new parcels vans stopped from 2000 after the separate Royal Mail and Parcelforce fleet organisations were merged.

Type 02

Type code 02 was allocated in 1971 to the Morris Minivan 45cf mailvan. With the end of Morris Minor production in spring 1972, the Minivan was adopted as the standard small mailvan and 2,301 were bought in 1972, followed by two smaller deliveries during the two following years. Small mailvans were tried again in the early eighties and Austin Metrovan 310 mailvans were bought in 1983 with serial numbers 3020001-428 with another six hundred and twenty the following year.

The Vauxhall Astramax 365 came to the end of production in 1993 and Royal Mail was keen to maintain a second supplier of small mailvans. The Vauxhall Combo with contemporary 'high-cube' styling was bought with an initial batch in 1993 serialled 3020500-3020599. Subsequent years saw 1,207 bought in 1994, 711 in 1995, 1,184 in 1996, 1,674 in 1997, 1,141 in 1998, 350 in 1999 and 500 in 2000.

The last six of the 1994 delivery were left-hand drive models, delivered as an experiment to see whether the safety advantage of not having to step out frequently on the road would be greater than the disadvantage of the left-hand driving position. They were tried out in North London and Tyneside areas and in East Anglia but without success. The experiment has not been repeated or extended.

Austin Metrovan EXI946 (3020161) at Belleek in Co. Fermanagh, Northern Ireland in June 1984. Royal Mail went through a phase in the mid-1980s of respraying vehicles in unrelieved red to highlight the Royal Mail lettering. Despite being only just over a year old when photographed, this one has evidently already been repainted. Mailvans in Northern Ireland have been registered with the distinctive registration marks of the province since October 1969 and continue to be so registered to this day. *P Eckersley*

Royal Mail continued a policy of dual-sourcing of small mailvans throughout the 1990s and turned to the original Vauxhall Combo in 1993 when the Astramax went out of production. This design of Vauxhall Combo was bought by Royal Mail between 1993 and 2000. Vauxhall Combo P946WWT (6021130) shows evidence of its rural deliveries when seen in Helmsley Market Place, North Yorkshire in October 1999. *D Longbottom*

Vauxhall Motors announced in November 2002 that it had secured an order from Royal Mail to supply up to 20,000 Vauxhall Combo vans over the following five years. An initial batch with 1.7 litre diesel engines was delivered in the first half of 2003 numbered 2020001-2022130, and further batches of 5,404 followed in 2003-04 and 4,425 in 2004-05 with a change of engine to the 1.3 CDTi diesel. The 2005 order started with serial 5020175 and some of the delivery is replacing earlier Combos as they reach twenty-seven months of service. It is expected that Royal Mail's small van fleet will be almost exclusively Vauxhall Combo during 2006 as a result of the replacement of the last Ford Escorts and Peugeot Partners.

In addition to the standard diesel-engined mailvan with type code 02, there have been smaller batches of dual petrol/lpg vans (type code 06), vans for Post Office Ltd (type code 21), vans for the Romec facilities management joint venture (type code 52), four-seat crewbuses (type code 89) with a first batch of four-seat postbuses (type code 76) delivered in November 2005.

Types 03 and 04

Type code 03 was allocated in 1971 to the Ford Anglia 50cf mailvan, bought by the GPO as an alternative to the Morris Minor between 1964 and 1968.

The next use of code 03 was in 1981 when it was used for a batch of forty-six Honda CB250RS-A motorcycles used for Expresspost services. 1982 delivery was of a further twenty-one Hondas (five more CB250s, eleven CD200TBs, and five CG125KCs). Two more Honda CB250RS and a single Suzuki GSX250E2 came in 1984, while 1985 saw twenty Kawasaki 250S Scorpion motorcycles followed by two more in 1986. Hondas returned to favour with 27 VT500 motorcycles with serial numbers 8030451-477, the serial numbers being chosen so that the registration numbers and serials could be the same. Nine Kawasaki GT550 and two Honda 125s were bought in 1990 and seven Kawasaki GT550G arrived in 1994. Five Honda NTV650T motorcycles arrived in 1995, eleven Kawasaki Z550s in 1996 and five Honda NT650V motor cycles followed in 1999. Fourteen Honda NT650V Deauville motorcycles were bought in June 2001 but these were withdrawn in 2003. Virtually all the motorcycles have been used on courier type work and most have been based in central London. Two Honda Dylan motorcycles were bought for January 2005 for Sameday deliveries in central London but were given type code 68.

Peugeot Partner vans were bought by Royal Mail between 1998 and 2001. The four battery-electric Peugeot Partners in Coventry new in 1999 remain in service after five and a half years in contrast to the normal life of a comparable diesel-engined van being between 2 years 3 months and 4 years. Pictured at Coventry Mail Centre in November 2004 is W627VLO (9041001). Note the special *ELECTRIC* lettering carried on the bonnet of these vehicles. *D A Cott*

Peugeot Partner LK02CPO (1040589) from the final 2001 delivery of these mailvans pictured at Corwen in May 2005. Note the bilingual Welsh livery *POST BRENHINOL*. *D Longbottom*

Type code 04 was allocated in 1971 to the famous Morris Minor 50cf mailvan, the last of which were delivered in 1972. In parallel with the purchase of the Austin Metrovan mailvans in 1983, the Post Office also tried out the petrol-engined Ford Fiesta and fifty-one were supplied in 1983 numbered 3040001-51.

Recent use of code 04 has been on the Peugeot Partner mailvan, the first of which were supplied in 1998 numbered 8040001-450, followed by batches of seven hundred and eight in 1999, five hundred and fifty-three in 2000 and eight hundred and sixty-seven in 2001. The final 2001 batch of Peugeot Partners was being replaced by Vauxhall Combos at the end of 2005. Nine of the 1999 delivery were battery-electric powered, four based in Coventry and the remainder in central London. Maintenance of the batteries has proved problematic and those in London have been replaced by standard diesel vans.

Types 05 and 06

Type code 05 was allocated in 1971 to the Morris J4 150cf mailvan and these were bought by the Post Office (with Austin-Morris badging) until production ceased in spring 1974.

The only other use of code 05 was a batch of five Freight-Rover Sherpa 350s with aluminium coachbuilt bodywork bought in 1985 for use as 500cf parcels vans in Northern Ireland, while a single Vauxhall Astravan Envoy was tried at Grange-over-Sands and Preston.

Type code 06 was first used in 1973 for five hundred of the newly introduced Morris Marina mailvan. Initially these vans were classified as 50cf mailvans, the same as the earlier Morris Minor, but the design was later reclassified as 80cf capacity. Another three hundred and twenty-nine Morris Marinas followed in 1974. The Morris Marina was chosen as the standard small mailvan in 1979 and large batches were supplied in the subsequent three years including 2,607 of the restyled BL Ital 440 van. A final batch of 780 Itals was delivered in 1983.

Morris Marinas and the restyled Morris Ital were bought by Royal Mail between 1979 and 1983. Morris Marina mailvan DTD399W (0060220), new in 1980, was photographed in Bolton in June 1983. Note the non-standard Royal Mail Special Services lettering combined with Datapost lettering on the cab doors and the Bolton telephone number. *P Eckersley*

A single Vauxhall Astra Envoy van with petrol engine and automatic transmission was obtained from City Motors of Oxford in November 2000 for use by a postman-driver with a disability. Initially X953OFC (0050001) was allocated to Grange-over-Sands but was later transferred to Preston where it was photographed in January 2005 immediately prior to withdrawal and sale. It had travelled 68,185 miles by the time it was auctioned in March 2005. *C M Hogan*

Over the years, the Post Office has carried out many experiments with alternative fuel technologies, the earliest back in 1928-29 in Leeds using Electromobile chassis imported from the USA. The early 1980s saw the conversion of substantial numbers of Morris Marinas to operate on both petrol and liquid petroleum gas (lpg) but the adoption of diesel fuel from 1985 put an end to lpg experiments. A further large-scale trial of lpg propulsion started in 2003 with the purchase of one hundred and forty-eight vehicles for use in central London and Perth. Seventy-nine of the vehicles are Vauxhall Combo vans, almost identical to the standard diesel vans, and these have serial numbers 2062001-79.

Types 07 and 08

Type code 07 was first used in 1972 for the first batch of Puch MV50 mopeds for use on letter delivery work, and further batches were bought until 1979.

The Mercedes-Benz Vito 108D was tried out in March 1999 as an alternative to the LDV Pilot and the Ford Transit with a trial batch numbered 8070001-39. Two further small batches of ten and thirty-one followed in 1999 and 2000.

Type code 08 was first used in 1975 for the first batch of Sherpas bought by the Post Office and deliveries of Sherpas and its successor, the LDV Pilot, as a 150cf mailvan have taken place annually from 1979 to 2002. The Sherpa, introduced in 1975 was an updated version of the BMC J4 design, first bought by the GPO in 1961 for use as a 150cf mailvan, with the engine moved forward from the cab into a bonnet. With the creation of Freight-Rover as a separate division in 1981, the Leyland name was replaced by Freight-Rover from the 1981 delivery. The original Sherpa design lasted until 1982 when the first facelift, with a smart new nose and a Range-Rover style grill, was given the title Sherpa K2. Another facelift in 1989 (and the sale of Freight-Rover to DAF in 1989) saw the Sherpa name dropped and deliveries from 1990 were badged Leyland-DAF 200 vans, although they continued to be universally known within the Post Office as the Sherpa.

Early Freight-Rover Sherpa 150cf BBJ238Y (2081185) from 1982 was photographed at Diss workshop in August 1989. In the background, Ford Escort B852DEV (5870066) receives some attention. *D A Cott*

The stylish Mercedes-Benz Vito was bought in small numbers between 1998 and 2000. Vito 150cf T241JHE (8070007) was photographed in Manchester in June 1999. *P Eckersley*

Illustrating the final deliveries of LDV Pilots is Y805BOA (1080084), photographed at Tunbridge Wells workshop in October 2001. Note the addition of the Royal Mail internet address to the livery. The vehicle features the new style registration plates with changed font introduced by the licencing authorities in readiness for the new registration format which commenced in September 2001. *D A Cott*

This view allows a comparison between the standard LDV Pilot R514UOP (7080499) and the alternative Ford Transit M499UWR (4090055) at Sheffield Mail Centre in May 1999. From October 1969 until 1997, mailvans were registered by the local operator after delivery while after that date, the manufacturer registered the vans before delivery, except those destined for Northern Ireland. The Transit was registered by Royal Mail North East division and the Pilot was registered by LDV. *M W Skillen*

Following the collapse of Leyland-DAF in 1994, the Washwood Heath van business was bought from the receivers in a management buyout and it assumed the name LDV. In 1996, another facelift saw the LDV 200 van became the LDV Pilot. In addition to its use as a 150cf mailvan, Sherpas and Pilots have also been bought as postbuses, crewbuses and postal engineering vans, as described later in this Handbook.

The total number of vans supplied as a 150cf mailvan is impressive: 875 in 1975; 948 in 1979; 1,120 in 1980; 1,008 in 1981; 1,502 in 1982; 700 in 1983; 1,187 in 1984; 577 in 1985; 665 in 1986; 1,287 in 1987; 808 in 1988; 1,963 in 1989; 2,148 in 1990; 1,743 in 1991; 445 in 1992 (including a single left-hand drive van as an experiment); 1,154 in 1993; 1,028 in 1994; 630 in 1995; forty 200s and 732 Pilots in 1996; 794 in 1997; 783 in 1998; 1,050 in 1999; 720 in 2000; 682 in 2001 and finally, 505 in 2002. In addition, Parcelforce bought four in 1989 and two Pilots in 2000 giving a total of 25,100 vans. Diesel engines are standard on this size of mailvan, while the traditional sliding door was replaced by a standard slam door from 1990. A minority of vans have shutters at the back instead of slam doors, while an additional nearside sliding door has been standard from 1999.

Royal Mail decided that it needed a larger capacity van and the new Ford Transit 260 has been the standard mailvan since 2003 in this size with a capacity of 225cf.

The Mailvan Handbook

Type 09

Type code 09 has had two uses since 1974. It was used between 1974 and 1978 for the Commer and Dodge Spacevan but these proved universally unpopular with drivers and mechanics on mailvan duties.

In 1987, the code was reallocated to the Ford Transit 150cf mailvan when a small batch of six with side doors to complement a larger order for thirty Transit 350cf models. A further batch of fifty followed in 1989 and these featured a rather unwieldy offside sliding cab door conversion. Another hundred, but with standard hinged doors came in 1992, two hundred in 1994, twenty-seven in 1996, eighty-nine in 1998, thirty in 1999, twenty-six in 2000. The breakthrough for Ford came in 2003, after Royal Mail decided it needed a larger van than the 150cf standardised on since 1961 and the new front-wheel drive Transit T260 was bought with a rated capacity of 225cf. Some 998 were supplied by Ford to Royal Mail in 2003 followed by a batch of seven hundred and eighty-three in 2004. A further large delivery was in progress during 2005.

When originally delivered, the fifty Ford Transit 150cf vans were fitted with a slam door on the nearside and a sliding door on the offside. The extra width, particularly of the runner at the top of the door, proved very vulnerable to damage and slam doors were quickly substituted. Policy has now changed and sliding doors are no longer specified for mailvans to overcome the tendency for them to be driven with the door open. Norwich's H234DRT (9090046) is pictured visiting Diss when new for staff training prior to the application of full livery. *D A Cott*

Type 10

Type code 10 has been used exclusively for Land Rover mailvans from 1971. The first Land Rover mailvans were bought by the GPO in March 1952 for use at Campbeltown and small numbers were bought each year for use on difficult terrain. The Post Office continued the tradition through the 1970s, while the numbers bought reduced sharply after 1980. The Land Rover has proved to be an expensive vehicle to operate on mailvan work, and alternatives such as standard mailvans fitted with limited-slip differentials have replaced Land Rovers on many of their traditional duties.

Deliveries in recent years have been limited to forty-five in 1990, seven in 1992, six in 1995 and seven in 1997. The adoption of the Vauxhall Brava in 2000 for these duties was expected to spell the end of Land Rover purchases but a single Land Rover was supplied in 2002, MK52YZL (2100001), for use at Todmorden. The once large fleet is now reduced to one in Wales, three in Scotland and a handful in Northern England.

The majority of the surviving Land Rovers and the Vauxhall Bravas from 2000 are expected to be replaced by a batch of nineteen Renault Kangoo 4x4 mailvans due for delivery in November 2005 with serial numbers 5100011-29, the first allocation of type code 10 to other than Land Rovers.

In addition to the use of Land Rovers as standard mail vans, a number were purchased for postbus use while redundant Land Rovers make excellent recovery vehicles at garages and workshops.

The majority of Ford Transit T260s supplied since July 2003 have had standard Ford unglazed rear slam doors. Some areas prefer to have rear roller-shutters instead of slam doors and this view of LD53BBN (3090688) shows the distinctive rear end of these vans. The Transit was photographed in Perth in April 2004 and illustrates the Scottish livery with the King's cypher. *D M Hinde*

Land Rover G949OUG (9100109) was new at Halifax in May 1990, but it later moved to Hebden Bridge where it was photographed in September 1992. This duty was replaced by another Land Rover in July 1996 and is expected to be replaced very shortly by a Renault Kangoo 4x4 crewbus. *P Eckersley*

The last Land Rover bought by Royal Mail was MK52YZL (2100001), a standard Defender 90 TD5 registered by Williams of Manchester, and based at Todmorden for use on the rough terrain in the area. Contrast this livery with the earlier van; it has a non-standard white roof, as well as the yellow stripes not normally carried by Land Rover mailvans. Future purchases of Land Rovers will depend on the suitability of the Renault Kangoo 4x4. *M W Skillen*

Type 11

The GPO bought three small batches of Austin Gipsy 60cf mailvans for comparison with the Land Rover, the last in 1967. The survivors were allocated code 11 in 1971.

Mailcars are used extensively by continental postal administrations but they had not been tried by the Post Office before 1983. In addition to the batch of Ford Fiestas bought in 1983 (type code 00), there was a batch of fifty Ford Escort 1.3 petrol-engined three-door saloons bought for mail delivery work serialled 3110001-50.

A Vauxhall Brava was tried on several postbus routes in Scotland from October 1997 and was purchased in May 1998 and given serial 8110001. It was obviously considered a success and further Vauxhall Bravas were bought in 2000 and 2001 to replace the majority of the surviving Land Rovers. Type code 11 was then reserved for the postbus variant, while the mailvan type was allocated type code 12. The production versions were both 4x4 and 4x2 versions, and they feature an Island Plastics conversion, rather than the Truckman hardtop of the demonstrator. The 2000 deliveries were 0110001-17 (4x4) and 0111001-15 (4x2).

Also on order for November 2005 delivery was a batch of forty-five Renault Kangoo 4x4 personnel carriers, to replace the 2000 Vauxhall Bravas on postbus duties and upgrade a few crewbus duties to four-wheel drive vehicles. Serial numbers are 5110001-45.

Continental postal administrations are enthusiastic users of mailcars for postal deliveries. Royal Mail tried them in the 1983-1985 period, before reverting to vans for such duties. Ford Escort mailcar B949UCK (3110023) is shown at Scorton Post Office, Garstang, in September 1984. P Eckersley

Land Rovers are popular choices as recovery vehicles when their days as mailvans are over. H154VWX (0100056) was new at Long Preston (an outstation from Skipton) and later moved to Ribblesdale. It was later sent to Sheffield as a recovery vehicle, and was fitted with winch and towing equipment. *M W Skillen*

Vauxhall Brava 4x4 postbus X426AHT (0110011) is seen at Thurso in July 2001. The rear body has gull wings to the upper half and two long trays (nicknamed 'coffins' by the drivers) accessed via the drop-down tailgate. Longer and with poorer visibility than the Land Rover which it replaced, the Brava has reportedly not met with universal praise from drivers and it has proved to be a troublesome and expensive vehicle to keep in service. This postbus entered service as a reserve vehicle at Thurso in November 2000 but moved to the Halkirk to Altnabreac postbus service in August 2003 to replace the 4x2 Brava pictured overleaf. *M W Skillen*

One of the 2000 delivery of 4x2 postbuses, X416AHT (0111001) was deployed on the Halkirk to Altnabreac service in November 2000 but was replaced on the route in August 2003 by 4x4 postbus X426AHT (0110011). The 4x2 version can be most easily differentiated by the smaller wheels. It was then shipped to Omagh workshop in Northern Ireland and is now used as the recovery vehicle for the western part of the province, where it is better regarded than the Land Rover it replaced. The only modifications made to the postbus are the removal of the Post Bus lettering and the fitment of towbar and connections for the lowloader recovery trailer. Scottish livery with the King's cypher is retained. *C M Hogan*

The Vauxhall Bravas carry the standard mailvan livery, complete with yellow stripes. Gaelic livery is carried by 4x2 X404AHT (0121006), photographed at Balivanich Post Office in August 2001. The Scottish Crown was removed on arrival at Lochboisdale Workshop and the lettering Post Rioghail substituted. *D A Cott*

Type 12

The first use of type code 12 was in 1981 when production of the Leyland EA was drawing to a close at Bathgate and the Post Office looked around for a suitable alternative for the 240cf mailvan. Among the vehicles bought were fifty Bedford CF vans with high roof bodywork in 1981 and a single similar vehicle in 1982.

The code remained unused until 2000 when deliveries of the Vauxhall Bravas started. Instead of separating the 4x4 and 4x2 Bravas with different type codes, code 11 is used for the postbus variant and code 12 is used for the mailvan. The main difference between the two types is the livery carried, the mailvan carries the double yellow V-shaped lines while the postbus has a more restrained livery with Post Bus lettering on each passenger door.

Thirty-one 4x4 mailvans and seven 4x2 mailvans numbered 0120001-31 and 0121001-7 were supplied in 2000 converted by Island Plastics, followed by four more 4x4s, 1120001-4, with SVP conversions in 2001. They replaced Land Rovers on delivery routes in Scotland and Northern England with three allocated to less obvious routes for these vehicles with 4x4s at Banbury and High Wycombe and a 4x2 at West Row near Diss. The four bought in 2001 are allocated to Abergavenny, Pontypool, Dingwall and Leek. A five-year life is planned for these vehicles with Royal Mail.

A standard Vauxhall Brava 4x4 mailvan in English livery is X283ATC (0120024), seen at Whitby. This vehicle was expected to be replaced by a Renault Kangoo 4x4 mailvan in November 2005. *D A Cott*

Types 13 and 14

Type code 13 was first used in 1973, when production of the BMC EA (easy access) design had been suspended to allow its transfer from the Adderley Park factory in Birmingham to the Bathgate factory. The Post Office bought two-hundred Ford Transit 175s for use as 240cf mailvans. They were long wheelbase vans with standard height roofs.

The next big purchase of Transit mailvans was in 1981 when fifty Ford Transit 160s arrived in parallel with the Bedford CFs (type code 12). Like the Bedfords, the Transits were standard-length, high-roof vehicles. 1987 saw another batch of sixty Transits bought for evaluation. Fifty-four were 240cf mailvans, all with high-roof bodywork, and thirty had a nearside sliding door.

As part of the 2003 lpg trial mentioned under type code 06, thirty-eight Ford Transit lpg vans were ordered for use in central London but only two (2132001/2) were delivered and the remainder were cancelled and LDV Convoys substituted instead.

Type code 14 was first used in 1983 when the first of the larger Freight-Rover Sherpa K4 vans were bought by the Post Office. The Sherpa K4s featured an extra-high fibreglass roof (to allow postmen to stand upright safely inside the van) and rear shutter doors. They were rated at 320cf capacity.

One of the 1987 batch of fifty-four Ford Transit high-roof 350cf mailvans is E78OMM (7130030). New in 1988, it entered service with North East London postal district at Walthamstow and was later transferred to Royal Mail's repair depot at Chorley where it received the livery introduced in 1990 with the yellow stripes and cruciform device together with lettering advertising its depot. It survived the closure of the depot and was not sold by Royal Mail until January 2001. *M W Skillen*

A standard LDV Convoy 320cf from the 1999 delivery is V852LOA (9140126). New to Edinburgh in November 1999 it was photographed in that city the following July. The large E50 duty number in this style is a feature of mailvans in the Scottish capital and the Borders. *D Longbottom*

Quadrant, the Post Office's catering organisation, also used 320cf vans for a time. Illustrated is K626CEG (3140348) at Milton Keynes in May 1994. *J P Targett*

Sherpas, LDV 400s and LDV Convoys of 320cf capacity were purchased annually from 1983 to 2001. This 1987 Freight-Rover Sherpa 320cf, E922TNF (7142014) is seen at Hazel Grove, Stockport, in May 1990. The figure *2* as the fourth digit of the serial number denotes the side door fitment. *P Eckersley*

1986 saw the large Sherpa retitled as Sherpa 300 and 1990 deliveries saw the first labelled as the Leyland-DAF 400. Deliveries from 1996 were restyled and badged as the LDV Convoy.

The 1987 delivery included sixty-four with a nearside slam door. Fifty in 1988, 8142001-50, were taken on lease from Newsflow in September 1988 for a period of twelve months and were later purchased by the Post Office. They dated from 1986 and were part of a batch of one hundred and seventy-eight that formed the bulk of the fleet of Newsflow, an NFC subsidiary set up in early 1987 to distribute the Mirror Group's London newspaper, the London Daily News. The 1993 delivery included seven in white livery for use by Quadrant, the Post Office's catering organisation.

An initial delivery of seventy in 1983 was followed by large annual deliveries through to 2001. However, it is understood that the 320cf capacity is now being phased out and future replacements will be either 225cf or 400cf capacity.

Type 15

Type code 15 was allocated in 1971 to the BMC EA (Easy Access) design. The first of this design had been bought by the GPO in 1969 and, apart from the break of production in 1973, continued to be purchased until 1982 with BMC, Austin-Morris and Leyland badging.

The later ones had very short lives and most had been sold by the late 1980s.

The BMC EA design was first bought by the GPO in 1969. The Post Office continued to buy them in both 240cf and 360cf sizes, with the last arriving in 1982 with 'LEYLAND' badging. Illustrated is XPW445X (1151012) from the 1981 delivery at Norwich in June 1988. Note the strengthened windscreen and security grills on the cab doors. *R W Taylor*

Types 16 and 17

Type code 16 was allocated in 1971 to the survivors of the Morris LD design with factory-built 240cf bodywork, last bought by the GPO in 1968. These became extinct during the 1970s.

The type code was reissued in 1982 to a single batch of a hundred Freight-Rover Sherpas fitted with a Walker high-roof conversion to generate the necessary 240cf capacity. They were intended as a stopgap between the cessation of Leyland EA production and the first of the new wide-bodied Sherpas becoming available to the Post Office. The Walker conversions did not prove popular and some did not enter service for two years, while many others were quickly redeployed on 150cf duties and three were even changed into the 150cf series as 2081503-5.

Type code 17 was issued in 1971 to the high-roof version of the Austin-Morris EA rated at 360cf capacity. The type was purchased in 1971 and from 1973 to 1981 inclusive.

Its next use was a batch of fifty Iveco Daily 35.8 vans bought in 1994 numbered 4170001-50. They were not well received and withdrawals started in 1997, although a few survived into 2001.

An LDV Convoy demonstrator, BV51KLO, fitted with an LDV box body and a Del Slim Jim tail-lift was bought by Royal Mail in February 2004 and given serial number 3170001.

This Bradshaw Enviroman electric van was demonstrated to the Post Office in full Royal Mail livery at a Lorry Driver of the Year award. It has a 680kg payload and 80km radius and was used on trial from London's West Central delivery office before being returned to the manufacturer. No serial number is thought to have been allocated to L455VCE. Though none of this type were bought, six Bradshaw Club car trucks were put into use in Oxford in December 1999. *M W Skillen*

A single batch of Iveco Daily panel vans was bought in 1994 but the vehicles did not find favour, although the Iveco Daily chassis-cab is used for the larger 550cf mailvan (type code 62). Iveco Daily M592XBM (4170022) is seen at Brighton in September 1997. *D Longbottom*

LDV Convoy demonstrator BV51KLO, on long-term demonstration to Royal Mail as an alternative to the Iveco Daily chassis for the 550cf mailvan, was bought in February 2004 and allocated to Biggar where it was photographed in August 2004. *C M Hogan*

Type 18

In 1971 type code 18 was allocated to the survivors of the Morris LD that were fitted with 360cf coachbuilt bodywork bought by the GPO and the Post Office between 1960 and 1971.

With the impending cessation of production of the LD's successor, the EA design, the Post Office tried out the Dodge 50-series with a single vehicle in 1981 followed by a further one hundred and three in 1982.

A single Volkswagen 35 mail van, numbered 0180001, was tried in 1990. Meanwhile, Parcelforce identified the need for a more sophisticated collection and delivery vehicle and it developed the 530cf delivery van. The first example was 2185001, a Leyland-DAF 400 fitted with a Cartwright Luton body delivered in 1992. The following year saw a further two hundred and three similar vehicles with both Leyland-DAF and Iveco Daily chassis. The 1994 orders were divided between twenty Ford Transits walk-throughs with Anglian Majestic bodywork and one hundred and twenty-seven more LDVs with a further three hundred and twenty-seven LDV 400s in 1995.

1996 saw a change of purchasing policy and standard Iveco Daily vans with factory built walk-through bodywork were chosen from 1996 to 2001.

Dodge 50-series panel vans were bought as 360cf mailvans in 1982 after the Leyland 440EA had gone out of production and before the wide-bodied Sherpa was available. The first of the Dodge model, CFW400X (2180001) was photographed in Grimsby in April 1988. Although lettered 'Parcels', along with most of the larger mailvans in the 1980s, these vehicles were mainly used on letters work. *P Eckersley*

Parcelforce opted for a more sophisticated van for urban collection and delivery work in 1993 with a 'walk-through' capability and power-operated nearside cab door. Leyland-DAF 400 530cf parcel van L552MAO (3185054) was photographed in Carlisle in August 1998. *M D Street*

Iveco Turbo Daily 530cf V581GGS (9187182) is seen at the Parcelforce depot at Stourton near Leeds in March 2000. These vans also had an electrically operated nearside door. Note the cypher added to the standard Parcelforce Worldwide livery. *D Longbottom*

Type 19

Type code 19 was allocated in 1971 to the then largest size of rigid mailvan, the 600cf, irrespective of chassis manufacture. Purchasing policy favoured the Leyland Terrier to 1984, then its replacement in the Leyland range, the Roadrunner between 1984 and 1988, although small numbers of Ford Cargos were bought in 1983 and 1985. The 1988 and 1989 orders were divided between the Roadrunner and the Ford Cargo and the 1990 and 1991 orders were solely for the Cargo. A longer variant with a capacity of 740cf (type code 61) was introduced in 1987 and no further 600cfs were bought by Royal Mail after 1991. A single Volkswagen was tried at Aberdeen in 1991, while Parcelforce bought six Roadrunners in 1990.

A large number of different bodybuilders has been used over the years, including Bedwas, Besco, Locomotors, Papworth Industries, Pem Trailers, Tidd, Wilsdon and some built at the Post Office's own repair depots at Bamber Bridge, Chorley and Kidbrooke.

Code 19 was reused in 2004 with a batch of one hundred and ninety-seven LDV Convoy extra-long wheelbase vans replacing the Iveco Daily vans on Parcelforce Worldwide duties. These were followed by five hundred and forty-one Iveco Daily panel vans.

The first 600cf mailvans were delivered to the GPO in 1954 on Karrier chassis. The use of this size of van was extended considerably during the 1960s and 1970s with the switch of mails and parcels from rail to road. A longer body of 740cf capacity was specified from 1987 and no further 600cfs were bought after 1991. Leyland Terrier 600cf A632GBU (4190043) with Papworth Industries bodywork from the 1984 delivery was photographed at Radcliffe, near Manchester, in August 1985. *P Eckersley*

BC53BBX is one of the one hundred and ninety-seven extra-long wheelbase LDV Convoy 530cf delivered in the spring of 2004. It is seen in Doncaster in July 2004 and carries the latest version of the Parcelforce Worldwide livery, reflecting that the business now caters only for express parcels and a partnership with GLS for continental deliveries. *J Lillford*

After the LDV Convoys, Parcelforce Worldwide reverted to the Iveco Daily van for the bulk of its 2004-05 530cf parcels van requirement with a large delivery of 541 of the 35S12 model to replace earlier Iveco Dailys from the 1998 to 2001 deliveries. The main external difference between these vans and earlier Iveco Dailys (type code 18) is the deletion of the nearside powered cab door. KE54BZL (4195541) was new in January 2005, is based at the Stoke depot and was photographed at Buxton in August 2005. *D Longbottom*

Type 20

The first use of type code 20 was in 1972 when the Post Office bought a batch of one hundred and ten Commer KCBN4023 chassis and fitted them with 400cf bodies built at its Bamber Bridge repair depot.

Reorganisation of the Post Office in 1986 into separate Letters, Parcels and Counters businesses further separated the mail and parcels collection and delivery arrangements. A requirement was identified for a vehicle for Heavy and Large Consignments and this appeared as a large rigid box van with nearside shutter of 1000cf capacity built to a 2.5 metre body width. The first two, 5200001/2, were Leyland Roadrunners with Besco bodywork tried out initially at Cardiff and they were soon joined with a further hundred similar vans with serial numbers 6200001-100. These were unusual in being registered by British Leyland C707-806MCW in March 1986 at a time when virtually all vehicles were still being registered by the Post Office after delivery. A further 880 vans, this time on Ford Cargo 0813 chassis and with an assortment of bodybuilders, Besco, Papworth, Locomotors and Tidd followed in 1987 to create the new network that became known as Network Two within Parcelforce.

Illustrated here, Leyland Roadrunner C794MCW (6200088) with Tidd bodywork shows the bilingual Post Brenhinol Parseli livery. Use of Welsh in the lettering of parcels vans in Wales ceased when the Parcelforce identity was created in 1988, but a limited use of Welsh was reintroduced on new Parcelforce Worldwide vans in Wales in 2005. *P Eckersley*

D831 RNA (7200026), a Ford Cargo 1000cf with Besco bodywork, is seen in Wilmslow in November 1988 while carrying an experimental SuperService livery, Subsequently not adopted, the Parcelforce livery was used instead. *P Eckersley*

Royal Mail adopted type code 20 for a rigid mailvan operating at 14 tonnes rather than the 17 tonnes of the established type code 37. Leyland-DAF 55 R334HAV (7200003), based at Bradford, was photographed passing York station in September 1998. *D Longbottom*

Leyland-DAF 45 1000cf parcels van N712HKH (6207003) was new to Parcelforce Worldwide at Hull and later moved to Scarborough. It was then rebodied as a recovery vehicle based at Bradford workshop. Other than its serial number and 'VSW BFD' (Vehicle Services Workshop Bradford) lettering, it carries no indication of its Royal Mail ownership. It is pictured in Halifax in August 2004 returning Peugeot Partner crewbus LS51TEO (1890049) from Halifax to Bradford. *D Longbottom*

More 1000cfs followed in 1989 with a further one hundred and seventy-one vans including a batch of twenty AWD TL 8.14s with Bedwas bodywork, the only vehicles of this marque bought by the Post Office. The 1990 order for two hundred and sixty-seven included a batch of thirty MAN 8.150s with Tidd bodywork. The 1992 order was for six hundred and thirty-eight Leyland-DAF Roadrunners and ten Ford Cargos that largely replaced the original Ford Cargos. 1994 to 1996 and 1998 to 2001 saw further batches of 1000cfs, on Iveco Cargo, Leyland-DAF 45, MAN and DAF LF chassis, generally fitted with Cartwright bodywork.

The recent streamlining of Parcelforce Worldwide and the concentration on premium parcels has seen the need for 1000cf vans sharply reduced. Not being fitted with tail-lifts, they were not suitable for redeployment on Royal Mail duties and many have been sold, often with only two years' service.

Royal Mail used type code 20 from 1997 for 1400cf vans operating at 14 tonnes gvw which were designed to carry up to twenty-four York containers on Royal Mail duties or up to twelve rigid stackable containers used for Mailsort duties. Deliveries commenced in 1997 with seventeen Leyland-DAF 55.180s with Marshall bodywork. Nineteen similar vans followed in 1998 plus two model 55.180s fitted with Boalloy bodywork, one of which had curtain-sided bodywork for Mailsort duties. Ten more followed in 1999 and eleven in 2000, including two with rollerbed floors for use at Aberdeen on containerised mail carried by air.

Type 21

The Post Office has long had a requirement for vehicles with an enhanced level of security and this was traditionally provided by equipping standard mailvans with extra security measures (see the photograph of 1151012 on page 25). A purpose-built security van, numbered 5210001, was bought in 1975 on the Commer KC chassis.

Dodge 50-series chassis with bodywork by Papworth Industries, Bedwas and Truck Developments were favoured for these duties up to 1988, with Freight-Rover Sherpas fitted out by Johnson Engineering bought in 1987-88 and the first Mercedes-Benz vans, 809Ds also fitted out by Johnson, in 1988. Later the 811D or 814D chassis was specified. Larger vans, based on Ford Cargo or Mercedes-Benz 1820 chassis, have been purchased. The current choice of chassis includes the Vario, the Sprinter and the Atego, all from Mercedes-Benz, and fitted with Johnson bodywork similar in pattern to those bought by Brinks, Securitas and Securicor.

Mercedes-Benz 1820 L335FPG (3210575) is shown at Swindon's Open Day in July 1995. *M W Skillen*

Small vans were introduced in 1995 using Ford Escorts and these have been joined by Peugeot Partners and Vauxhall Combos. A further type, based on the Ford Transit 90T350 high-roof van, was introduced in 2002.

The Post Office cash operation is now a subsidiary of Post Office Ltd., the counters business, and vans are now painted in POST OFFICE livery.

Dodge 50-series E787HDX (4210053) with Papworth Industries bodywork is seen at Norwich in May 1988. This vehicle was a very late registration for a 1984 vehicle and it carries Royal Mail Parcels lettering, notwithstanding its use on cash handling.
R W Taylor

Mercedes-Benz 814 with Johnson bodywork Y532JUX (0210090), in a bilingual version of the latest "green sash" Post Office livery, and was photographed at Porthmadog in August 2001.
M W Skillen

The latest size of van operated by **Post Office Ltd** is the **Ford Transit** high-roof 90T350 van. DX54VBZ (4215022) from the 2004/5 order of thirty such vans was photographed in Stafford in August 2005.
D Longbottom

MAN replaced Iveco as the second choice for HGVs between 1997 and 2000 replacing the Cargo 740cfs and Eurotech artics. MAN 22-403 6x2 motive R484SLD (7230054) was photographed at Carlisle in August 1998.
M D Street

Types 22 and 23

Type code 22 was allocated in 1971 to the surviving Scammell Townsman and Karrier Bantam motive units bought by the GPO. The code has been used sporadically for yard shunters and two 1975 Leyland Chieftain motive units were renumbered 3220001/2 in 1983 for such duties.

Type code 23 was initially allocated to Ford D300 motive units bought in 1971 to replace these Scammell Townsman and Karrier Bantam motive units on short distance movements of trailers between customers, sorting offices and rail stations. Fords were favoured for these orders up to 1980 but for the final delivery in 1981, a batch of 30 Bedford TKs was supplied instead.

The code was reused in 1991 when seventy 38-tonne tri-axle motive units were bought for Mailsort work. They were made up of Leyland-DAF 95s numbered 1230001-40 and Seddon-Atkinson Stratos with Cummins 325 engines numbered 1230041-70. An Iveco Eurotech followed in 1992 with a batch of nineteen Eurotech 400s coming in 1993. The 1993 models proved unsatisfactory and they were superseded in December 1995 by nineteen replacements under warranty. Since then, purchases of this size of motive units have generally favoured Leyland-DAF or DAF, although MAN products were bought between 1997 and 2000 in small numbers. Current deliveries are DAF CF85.430 6x2 with ninety-six obtained in 2003 as a result of the transport reorganisation and the opening of the National Distribution Centre at Daventry with further batches in 2004 and 2005.

The Post Office tried a small number of Leyland Cruisers but decided to concentrate on the higher-capacity Roadtrain and Ford Cargo. This view shows C685JVX (5240139) at Norwich in May 1988.
R W Taylor

Type 24

Type codes 24 and 25 were allocated in 1971 to motive units with a capacity of up to 22 tons (24) and up to 32 tons gross weight (25). Increasing numbers of motive units and semi-trailers had been bought by the Post Office during the 1970-75 period, and the main use for these vehicles was as a result of the reorganisation of the parcels service with the creation of Parcel Concentration Offices and the transfer of trunking from rail to road. The majority of the motive units were of the 20/22-ton capacity type, with Commers, Dodges, Ford D-series and Leyland Chieftains specified in the Post Office's orders.

The 1980s saw the removal of the remaining parcels traffic from rail and the extension of road trunking as the Post Office mechanised its letters service and built new Automated Processing Centres (APCs) in many cities and larger towns. During the 1980s there was a move away from 20/22 ton artics to higher capacity and higher specification vehicles.

Motive units coded 24 were bought until 1985 and included Dodge Commandos, Ford Cargo and Leyland Chieftains.

The type code was reallocated in 1997 to dockspotters, when a batch of twenty Reliance-Mercury machines was bought for Parcelforce Worldwide use at its larger depots. A further batch of twenty, this time of Terberg manufacture, with Cummins B-series Elite engine and an Allison MT643 14-speed gearbox, arrived in 1999 for use at Parcelforce's Coventry Hub. For Royal Mail's National Distribution Centre at Daventry which opened in September 2003, a fleet of leased Terbergs in yellow livery is used for internal shunting of semi-trailers. The majority of the dockspotters operate solely within depots and most are not registered.

Reliance-Mercury dockspotter 7247007 pictured at the Yorkshire Parcel Centre at Leeds in March 2000, shunting a 1992 Cartwright 13-metre semi-trailer. Note that the shunter has been embellished with one of the gilt relief cyphers used on parcels vans in the late 1980s.
D Longbottom

Types 25 and 26

Type code 25 was allocated in 1971 to motive units with a capacity of up to 32 tons gross weight.

The Post Office initially favoured the Guy Big J for its early purchase of 32-ton motive units in the 1970s, having bought similar machines for its Supplies trunking fleet from the mid-1960s. The Guys gave way to the Leyland Marathon and the first Leyland Roadtrains were bought in 1981. 1982 saw a substantial delivery of fifty-three Leyland Roadtrains with Rolls-Royce RR265L engines while the majority of the 1983 delivery of sixty-three Roadtrains had Leyland engines. Other types were also tried including ten Foden Fleetmasters 3250004-13 with Cummins engines in 1983 and three trial units in 1985, one each of the Ford Cargo, Volvo FL7 and Leyland Cruiser.

Many of the type code 25 motive units, particularly those on parcels work, were licensed at 26 or 28 tonnes gross weight, and this was recognised in 1985 when a new code (26) was introduced to cover these units while existing vehicles were recoded. The 1986 delivery reflected this change with three hundred and thirty-five motive units bought that year with code 26, including seventy Ford Cargo units destined for the separate Network 2 operations being set up with the newly created parcels division to deal with heavy and large consignments.

Leyland Roadtrain 17-28 motive unit F273LFT (8260046) at Sunderland sorting office in October 1990 coupled to trailer 9280101 carrying the short-lived blue Mailsort lettering. Mailsort was replaced in 1991 by the brand STREAMLINE and this was carried on trailers for a couple of years before the lettering was hastily removed due to privatisation fears. Mailsort continues to be used by Royal Mail for marketing its bulk mail services. *D A Cott*

Another marque tried in the 1990s was Mercedes-Benz. Mercedes-Benz Actros 1831 R885LNK (7250008) was based at Peterborough and was photographed near King's Lynn in September 2000. *P Eckersley*

The current choice for motive unit is the DAF CF85 with the 4x2 variant forming the majority of recent deliveries. The majority of the Royal Mail trucking fleet was expected to comprise of such machines by the end of 2005, with the oldest less than three years old. Pictured at the National Distribution Centre at Daventry in May 2004, PO53UGZ (3250111), is coupled to a Cartwright double-deck semi-trailer 3310001 able to carry up to 75 York containers, as opposed to the 45 of a standard semi-trailer. *D A Cott*

Leyland-DAF 75 motive unit P868WWT (6250055), with leased semi-trailer, leaving York in March 1998. It was based at the Yorkshire Distribution Centre at Morley. *D Longbottom*

Other purchases in 1986 were two Volvos, ten Renault G260s, ten Seddon-Atkinsons as well as more Ford Cargos and Leyland Roadtrains. Similar purchases were made in 1987, while 1988 saw fifty-five Leyland Roadtrains for letters work licensed at 26 tonnes, seventy-three Leyland Roadtrains for standard parcels licensed at 28 tonnes and for Network 2, thirty-five Leyland Roadtrains, ten Mercedes-Benz Powerliner Twos and five MAN 17-292s with sleeper cabs. 1989 deliveries were dominated by more Roadtrains but some Leyland-DAF 95s, Iveco 190/32s, ERF and Seddon-Atkinsons were included in a delivery of 453 26/28-tonners and 32 32-tonners.

Royal Mail continued to favour Leyland-DAFs, generally the 75 type, but Parcelforce bought thirty-one Mercedes-Benz 1831s, forty Scania E113MA4X2R-320s and thirty-eight Iveco EuroTech 40034Ts as well in 1993. Eight Renault R340ti Highliners formed part of the 1995 Parcelforce delivery. MANs were bought by both Royal Mail and Parcelforce in the 1997 to 2000 period. 1998 saw the first batches of the DAF 85CF motive unit, the successor to the Leyland-DAF 75 and 80 models.

The 2003-04 delivery was for 270 DAF CF85.380 units serialled 3250092-361 in connection with the opening of the National Distribution Centre at Daventry. Deliveries in 2004 and 2005 saw the replacement of

The Mailvan Handbook

many earlier motive units, and on completion of these deliveries, the oldest motive units in Royal Mail service will date from 2003. These also operate at 38 tonnes gtw with the only distinction between those coded 23 and 25 being their three and two axle configurations. The last of the 2005 order feature a two position sliding fifth-wheel coupling to assist with coupling operations at depots.

The Post Office tried ten Foden Fleetmasters with Cummins engines in 1983. A624GBU (3260009) was photographed in Bolton in April 1987.
P Eckersley

Second-hand vehicles, other than demonstrators, are not common in the Post Office fleet. This Iveco-Ford Cargo, originally registered H156BJA (5265049), was bought in December 1995 from Exel Logistics where it was used on contract to Marks & Spencer in light green livery. The Post Office used it as a dockspotter by Parcelforce Worldwide at Peterborough where it was photographed in July 1999. Note the non-standard livery, the absence of registration plates and the name 'CHUNKS'.
M W Skillen

Types 27 to 34

Type codes 27 to 30 were allocated to semi-trailers and type code 31 was allocated to ISO Containers. Subsequently codes 31 to 34 have also been used for semi-trailers.

The initial allocation was type code 27 to semi-trailers of up to 650cf capacity, 28 for larger box semi-trailers, 29 for the 12.2m long skeletal semi-trailers and 30 for shorter skeletal semi-trailers.

500cf and 650cf semi-trailers were used with the small motive units (those coded 22 and 23). The batch of sixty-two Taskers trailers with Papworth Industries bodywork was bought in 1975. A batch of redundant National Carriers' trailers was bought in 1980 numbered 9270001-86 but twenty-eight of them were never used by the Post Office.

Purchases of larger semi-trailers (type code 28) in the early 1970s were mainly curtain-sided trailers of 1300cf capacity manufactured by Brockhouse with Longwell Green bodywork, Brockhouse/Marshall, Carrimore, Crane Fruehauf, Taskers/Longwell Green, Taskers/Marshall, and York/Boalloy. 1978 saw a move away from curtain-sided bodywork to a box van configuration, but the move towards higher capacity motive units meant that the last significant batch of 1300cf trailers was Tidds 8285001-114, bought by Parcelforce in 1988.

Green Post Office vehicles are not common but this livery is carried by this Schmidt 2016 road sweeper (5342000) used at the Purchasing & Logistics Service depot at Swindon. The gritter trailer carries serial 5342001. *M W Skillen*

Small batches have been bought in recent years, the most recent deliveries were 0285001-20 and 0286001 in 2000, but there are only about twenty-five of this size of trailer still in service.

The first ISO Containers were bought in 1970 and were used with skeletal semi-trailers, initially on foreign mails work, but from 1973 on parcels trunking duties as well. Skeletal trailers of 6.1m (20ft), 9.15m (30ft) and 12.2m (40ft) lengths were all bought up to 1985 of Brockhouse, Carrymaster, Crane-Fruehauf, Dayson, M & G, Merriworth, Scammell, and Taskers manufacture. The containers themselves were also bought between 1970 and 1985 in all three lengths, but only one type code (31) was allocated to all of them. Both Royal Mail and Parcelforce moved away from ISO Containers but there is still a handful of skeletals left in service.

Code 29 was used again in 2003 for a batch of Cartwright 13.4m box semi-trailers equipped with rollerbed floors for easier movement of small containers, such as those for foreign mail. Type code 31 is now used for double-deck trailers to resolve the conflicting use of code 33, but existing trailers have not been renumbered.

Type code 32 was introduced in October 1983 for tandem-axle semi-trailers of 12.2m length classified at 2250cf capacity. Small numbers of these longer trailers had been bought from January 1976 and the existing 12.2m trailers were recoded 32 in 1983. Thereafter the 2250cf 12.2m trailer became the preferred type for both letters and parcels. From 1994, the position with this type code became confused as Parcelforce adopted the longer 13.4m box as standard, but continued to use type code 32 for trailers, while Royal Mail bought similar trailers but allocated them code 33! This has continued with 2003-04 deliveries made up of 3326001-92 and 3330068-92, apparently identical Cartwright 13.6 metre trailers. Semi-trailers are now largely common-user across the Royal Mail businesses and those obtained in 2004 and 2005 were all coded 33. Worthy of mention are 7325001 and 8325101-8 which were standard Cartwright trailers but fitted with special lifting pockets for use on the London - Glasgow rail service, in piggyback mode. These were withdrawn in August 2002 and the trailers sold in January 2003.

Parcelforce adopted type code 33 for a small number of double-deck trailers, generally of Wilson manufacture. Royal Mail used the code from 1991 for its fleet of 13.4m tri-axle trailers used on Mailsort duties, the majority of which have curtain-sides. With the rationalisation of the logistics operation, type code 33 used for standard 13.6 metre semi-trailers manufactured by Cartwright – some have tail-lifts, others have lifting rear axles and some have curtain-sided bodywork.

Finally type code 34 was used in 2001 for a batch of Cartwright 13.4m tandem-axle semi-trailers.

Types 34 and 35

As already noted, type code 34 has been used by Parcelforce in 2001 for a single batch of semi-trailers.

The original use of type code 34 is on various mechanical aids including grass cutters and sweepers. Type code 35 is allocated to large fork-lift trucks powered either by diesel or lpg. Most fork-lifts are the smaller battery-electric type (type code 42) but the larger fork-lifts are to be found at Mailsort distribution centres for moving and loading the large cage containers used on this work. Boss, Hyster, Jungheinrich, Komatsu, Still and Yale are among the manufacturers who have supplied machines, but the current policy appears to be to lease these machines and contract their maintenance out to specialist firms.

Typical of the large diesel fork-lifts is this unregistered Boss QX20 4350008 which was photographed in Norwich during April 2002. *D A Cott*

Type 36

The only use of type code 36 is a MAN ECO.370 17.322 FLDN chassis cab fitted with Cartwright demounting equipment and RSG tail-lift numbered 4360001 with Cartwright DMDB18A drawbar trailer 4361001 and four container boxes 4362001-4. It was exhibited at the Lorry Driver of the Year final at MIRA in September 1994 but it is believed never to have entered service in its intended form as it met stiff trade union opposition in Liverpool. It was later transferred to Swindon and is thought to have been used as a standard box van without its drawbar trailer.

This MAN chassis-cab with container and drawbar trailer was photographed at the Lorry Driver of the Year final at MIRA in September 1994. It was later registered M430TRF. *M W Skillen*

Illustrating contrasting body styles on different vehicles from the same batch are these two Leyland-DAF 60.180s with Cartwright bodies – on the left M479 SOJ (4370017) with high curtain-sided bodywork used for bulk mail trunking and on the right M685 ROK (4370007) used on conventional letters work. Both were based at Northampton and were photographed at the Lorry Driver of the Year finals in 1995. *M W Skillen*

Type 37

The need for a larger rigid mailvan led to the allocation of type code 37 in 1984. The first vehicles with this code were 4370001/2, Leyland Freighters with Besco GRP bodywork rated at 900cf Another four similar vehicles followed in 1986, while 1987 saw the arrival of 7370001, a Dodge Commando with bodywork built at the Post Office's repair depot at Bamber Bridge. More Commandos followed in 1988, while 1989 saw a significant expansion in the use of these vehicles with twenty-six being purchased for Royal Mail use and ten for Parcelforce. Most of these arrivals were rated at 17-tonnes and had longer bodies with a capacity of 1400cf. The 1990 arrivals included ten Iveco Cargo chassis, while the four for Parcelforce, with Leyland-DAF 2700ATi chassis-cabs were for use with sixteen 1400cf demountable bodies.

The creation of a separate network for Mailsort distribution led to more use of this size of mailvan including some with curtain-sided bodywork. The Leyland Freighter was phased out in 1991 and its successor, the Leyland-DAF 60-180, was used for the 17-tonne 1400cf van. With an overall height of 3.5m they were found to be too tall to access some premises, so the 1991 order included two Leyland-DAF 50-160 chassis with bodywork 300mm lower and operating at 12.5-tonnes gross weight.

The current choice for 17-tonne mailvans is the DAF LF55.220 chassis with a number of different body styles. Illustrated here is curtain-sided MF51HKN (1371008), new to the Essex distribution centre in December 2001 for bulk mail work, and photographed at Chelmsford in May 2005. *C M Hogan*

Photographed at Diss during February 1991, Iveco-Ford Cargo H36FNK (0370004L) carries Tidd bodywork. The use of L suffixes in serial numbers, to denote leased vehicles, was short-lived. *D A Cott*

A significant order for this size of mailvan was a batch of one hundred and twenty-three for Royal Mail duties bought in 1995. They were used both for Mailsort work and for trunking of standard mails, marking the start of the recent transfer of mails from rail to road.

From 1997, vehicles with curtain-sided bodywork used on Mailsort work, were differentiated by having 1 as the fourth digit of their serial number. Vans operating at 14 tonnes gvw were given a separate type code (20) from 1997, but existing vehicles were not renumbered. Capacity of the standard van was uprated to 1750cf in 1998, when the height of the bodywork was increased to give an overall height of 4m. This allowed the vans to carry either twenty-four York trolleys or twenty Mailsort containers double-stacked in the bodywork.

The DAF LF55 succeeded the DAF 55.210 from 2001 and three DAF LF75 6-wheelers, numbered 1373004-6, were bought for Mailsort duties based at Hatfield. A further eleven similar vehicles were delivered in 2004. The opening of the National Distribution Centre at Daventry resulted in the purchase of one hundred and fourteen DAF LF55s with van bodywork in 2003, as well as thirty with Cartwright curtain-sided bodywork for Mailsort duties. Further similar vehicles were delivered in 2004 and 2005.

Type 38

Post Office electric tractors towing trolleys around rail stations have been a familiar sight until recently. Type code 38 is allocated to these machines and small batches of electric tractors of Crompton Electricars, Hamech, Harbilt, Lansing-Bagnall, Montgomerie-Reid, Reliance-Mercury, Wessex manufacture have been bought over the years. Policy changed recently and electric tractors are no longer bought outright but leased instead.

Also coded 38 were the larger electric trucks able to carry mail as well as tow trolleys. They tended to be used where the station and the sorting office were close together and they were a familiar sight in larger cities. Two of the 1986 batch of twenty-eight Electricars C5000 4-wheel tow-tractors, 6380045/6, were later converted to Electric Delivery Trucks with an enclosed body with a nearside sliding door.

Six Bradshaw Club Car 'Carry 2' 4-wheel battery-electric vans were tried at Oxford for city centre mail deliveries in 1999, one has subsequently been transferred to Abergavenny, where it replaced the pedestrian truck used on town centre deliveries.

Preston named its station tractors after ships lost in the Falklands War. A438JFR (2380036) named 'Antelope' was photographed at Preston rail station in August 1986. *P Eckersley*

Use of Royal Mail electric road trucks on public highways was a frequent sight, particularly in northern England. B757GFE (5380060) makes the short trip from Lincoln sorting office to the station in September 1987. *P Eckersley*

Stansted Airport has become a busy hub for onward internal and international mail trunked in from as far afield as Bournemouth. The mail is loaded into a fleet of five trailers *(see page 58)* and towed airside by leased Lansing PE250 TriACtive tractors numbered RM1-3 and elderly Electricars 2380058. They are seen in company with Escort P512JAV (6872467), which was fitted with airside requirements including a flashing light bar and fire extinguisher. *D A Cott*

Royal Mail tried six Bradshaw Club Car battery-electric trucks at Oxford where they are used in the pedestrianised areas of the city centre. V420SEG (9389006) was later transferred to Abergavenny where it has been used to replace a life-expired pedestrian-controlled electric truck (PEDT) on town centre deliveries. It was photographed at its new home in September 2003. Royal Mail is understood to be considering buying up to 15,000 powered delivery trolleys for urban mail delivery in the next five years and it is trialling a MagiCexpress electric trolley (manufactured by Expresso-Deutschland GmbH) with a capacity of 150kg at the Swindon delivery office. *P J Relf*

Type 39

The GPO first tried out pedestrian-controlled electric trucks on delivery work in 1954 and bought large numbers from 1957. They have large sliding doors on both sides and internal shelving for efficient carriage of parcels for delivery. Their principal use was on town and city centre parcels deliveries where the sorting office was within reasonable walking distance of the delivery area.

Electrics tend to have long lives and many of the trucks from GPO days were still in service in the early 1980s when a limited refurbishment programme took place in 1981-82. A big batch of one hundred and two new trucks was bought in 1985 comprising sixty Harbilt 735 trucks of traditional design and forty-two built by Wingrove & Rogers with a more modern angular design. Five Electricars trucks followed in 1991 numbered 1390171-5, but no further machines of this type have been bought since. There were just nine still owned by Royal Mail in September 2003.

Three redundant PEDTs from Norwich, C598LNV (5390004), C150TJU (5390001) and D101RHK (5390066) were seen at Diss in October 1990. The last is of Wingrove & Rogers manufacture with the other two built by Harbilt. Of interest is the double mirror fitted to C598LNV. *D A Cott*

PMG814E (1390032) started life in 1967 as a standard PEDT and was later converted to a *Postman Pat* van for use at shows and events. It was photographed in Norwich in June 1995, loaded on publicity trailer 9840501. *D A Cott*

Types 40 and 41

Type code 40 was allocated in 1971 to a different design of pedestrian-controlled truck, the open trucks normally used at stations for carrying loose mailbags delivered to or received off trains. They were bought in much smaller numbers than the delivery trucks, but seven Harbilt 725 trucks were bought in 1982, followed by small numbers in the following three years. None remains in service with Royal Mail.

York containers, known as such because they were first trialled at York mail centre, were introduced in 1992 and Royal Mail has bought 340,000 of them from manufacturer Bekaerts.

Type code 41 was introduced in 1995 for the York Lifter used at stations to bridge the gap between the platform and the floor of the trains. They were really mobile ramps and bridging boards and were deployed on platforms to load and unload York trolleys from mail trains. Thirty-nine of Jungheinrich manufacture were supplied in 1995 and a further sixty-seven followed in 1996. The end of the Railnet operation has rendered most of these machines redundant.

Less numerous than the PEDT was the PEST used on passenger stations to transport mailbags from trains to road vehicles or sorting offices. They shared a common chassis but featured an open rather than a box body. One of the later machines, XPN7Y (2400007) from 1982, was photographed on charge at Three Bridges station in December 1984. *M W Skillen*

The task of moving large numbers of Yorks relatively long distances on rail platforms at Railnet terminals and in the largest handling centres was carried out in several ways. This view shows an unpowered York Mover trailer out of use at Crewe workshop in July 2005 after seeing service at Crewe rail station. This has a ramp at the rear to load the Yorks and a standard AST-type front end to allow towing by an electric tractor. The design presumably proved impractical as it had limited capacity and was too unwieldy for rail platforms. A large number of York Purpose Built Trailers was later supplied by AMSS, designed to be towed in long rakes behind a tractor each can carry two containers and load directly into a rail van. The Rail Terminals then received driver-ridden Boss York Movers, able to carry five Yorks at speed, although these are leased and maintained under contract and so do not carry traditional serials. *C M Hogan*

Jungheinrich supplied purpose-built York Lifters in 1995 and 1996 to allow York containers to be transferred between station platforms and trains. The solid-tyred battery-electric machine is steered by a tiller that also incorporates a standard hitch to allow it to be towed by an electric tractor if required. It would be parked adjacent to the door of the rail van, the cage raised hydraulically, the 750mm side ramp lowered to the van floor and the metre-long rear ramp lowered to the platform. The York can then be pushed onto the 1080mm diameter turntable in the cage floor, turned through ninety degrees and rolled into the van. York Lifters were designed as mobile ramps and were not intended to be moved with a York in the cage. The photograph shows Carlisle's York Lifter 3 (serial 6410063) on the station platform in August 2002, between duties in the company of an electric tractor and several empty Yorks. *M W Skillen*

Types 42 and 43

Type code 42 was allocated in 1971 to a range of mechanical aids including battery-electric fork-lift trucks and pallet trucks. These machines were generally bought for specific sites with different specifications. A total of 600 were bought between 1982 and 1998, but recent policy is to lease the trucks (on a lease and maintenance arrangement) rather than buying them outright.

The 1994 deliveries included twelve Jungheinrich order pickers for use at the warehousing operation at Swindon.

The original use of type code 43 was for eleven battery-electric mailvans from 1967 and 1969 of Smiths or Crompton-Leyland manufacture. In 1995, the code was reallocated to pallet trucks but the only significant delivery was a batch of twenty-one bought in 1996.

The lighter battery-electric powered fork-lifts are coded 42, although current policy is for them to be leased and their maintenance to be contracted out to specialist suppliers, and hence do not carry conventional serial numbers. 4420031, a Coventry-Climax 1800kg capacity truck new in 1984, was still in use by Parcelforce Worldwide at Stourton when it was photographed in March 2000.

This Lansing pallet truck was photographed at the Swindon warehouse in June 1996. *M W Skillen*

Type 44

Type code 44 was allocated in 1971 to All-Steel trailers used at stations, airhubs and sorting offices for the movement of mailbags. They are capable of being coupled to form 'trains' and were normally moved by electric tractors. FMW Engineering, Curtsons of Radstock, Simon Reeve, the Bamber Bridge repair depot all built trolleys to the same basic design. The move away from loose mailbags to York trolleys for mail transport has substantially reduced the number of All-Steel trailers in use and the closure of the Travelling Post Office and other rail services has further reduced the requirement for them.

Type code 44 has also been used on redundant former BR 'BRUTE' trolleys bought by the Post Office over the years (the last in 1987) and repainted red.

Four of the five airside trailers used at Stansted Airport are in red Royal Mail livery, while the fifth is dedicated to Irish Mails and appropriately painted green. None has been allocated a serial number and all are known simply by their chassis numbers. Number 22752 is pictured undergoing routine maintenance at Harlow workshop in August 2000. *D A Cott*

Arran hopper trailer at Brodick brings mail off 7.55 am ferry behind H411BSA (0082734) in August 1995. *D A Cott*

The All-Steel Trailer was developed after the Second World War as the most common method of moving bagged mail on rail stations, where the mailvans were not able to pull alongside the trains. The front handle couples to the standard hitch on electric tractors and the back of other ASTs, allowing them to be formed into rakes. Originally known as Turntable Platform Trailers and numbered in a special TT series, deliveries from around 1968 were given normal trailer serials. ASTs have been built by a variety of manufacturers over the years, including some by the Central Repair Depot at Bamber Bridge. They are unpainted galvanised steel to the same basic design, with a slatted floor, slightly raked ends, open sides and pneumatic tyres. Various methods of retaining the load have been used including panelling in one side, fitting chains, fabric curtains, nets, and hinged or folding sides. The photograph was taken airside at Liverpool's John Lennon Airport in April 2001 and shows rakes of ASTs on the apron awaiting their next duty, with the runway behind and the River Mersey and Ellesmere Port in the distance. Number 49 in the left foreground has serial 1440160 and is a Simons Reeve example from 1991, which make up the majority of the fleet here. The one on the right foreground is from a batch of twenty without serials built by Owen Holland (Engineering) Ltd of Blandford in Autumn 2000 to replace earlier examples at Speke. *M W Skillen*

Types 45 to 50

Type code 45 was allocated to the original Post Office trolley developed in the late 1960s and known as the POTU (Post Office Trolley Universal). These wheeled trolleys were developed as part of the early concentration of parcels and their transport in semi-trailers and containers. The last batch bought was 1450001-70, the Mk IV version, built by Warwick Production. They were superseded by the MATE with type code 48.

Code 45 was thus vacant and the development by Freight-Rover of a battery-electric version of the K2-series Sherpa, the Post Office bought two in 1982 for evaluation. Developed in conjunction with Lucas Chloride EV Systems, the Sherpa Electric offered a payload of 950kg for its gvw of 3.5 tonnes with all of its 36 six-volt batteries located underneath the van's floor. A larger trial was inaugurated in 1984 with Bedford CFs 4450001-40 and Sherpas 4450041-80, but it was found that the batteries could not provide sufficient charge for an entire day's work, particularly in hilly areas. Another trial vehicle was 1454999, a Smith's electric with Cartwright bodywork, tried out by Parcelforce Worldwide in central London in 2001, now thought to have been returned to the manufacturer.

The Post Office even operates a milk float. 1460001 was bought second-hand from Co-op Dairies and is used at Purchasing & Logistic Services site at Swindon. *M W Skillen*

Royal Mail operates three of Ford's latest van, the Transit Connect, having lost out on the main order to the Vauxhall Combo. LC53GTZ (3490002) is based in London (note the Congestion Charge sticker in the windscreen) but was photographed in Windsor in September 2005. *F J Weston*

Type code 46 was allocated to a pedestrian electric truck and a single Lansing-Bagnall 2460001 was bought in 1982 for use at Chester. The code was used again in 1991 when a Morrison-Electricar E11G milk float was bought from Co-op Dairies and was allocated number 1460001.

Type code 47 was allocated in 1972 to a container known as the MACE (Mails All-purpose Container Equipment). One thousand one hundred and twenty were bought in 1972-73 though none subsequently; nor has there been any further use of this type code.

Type code 48 was allocated in 1972 to a trolley known as the MATE (Mails All-purpose Trailer Equipment). These superseded the POTU on parcels work and were bought in large numbers between 1972 and 1989. They featured a steel base, similar in design to the B.R. BRUTE, but with heavy plywood sides and a single 'stable-door' arrangement on one side.

Type code 49 remained vacant until 2003 when it was allocated to three Ford Transit Connect T200 mailvans bought for special duties. The Transit Connect is the successor to the Ford Escort and its upright design with greater ground clearance and more robust construction would appear to have made it ideal for Royal Mail delivery duties. Fords appears to have tried hard to persuade Royal Mail to buy Transit Connects, with several demonstrators in full livery made available, but the Vauxhall Combo was chosen instead in 2002 as Royal Mail's standard small mailvan.

Type code 50 was allocated to Platform Lift trailers, with two supplied in 1987 and eight more in 1988.

Types 51 to 53

Types 51-58 were all allocated to vehicles used on postal engineering duties. In GPO days, postal engineering was carried out for local Head Postmasters by the local telephone area, but increasing mechanisation of postal operations led to a separate postal engineering function being created in each region in 1968. Green telephone vehicles were repainted overall red with appropriate lettering. In 1971, the livery was brightened up with the addition of a white waistband, and through the 1970s until the creation of British Telecommunications in 1981, the vehicles used were similar in specification to contemporary telephone vans.

The white waistband changed to yellow in 1982 and the lettering became Post Office Engineering at the same time. In 1989, these services were reorganised into a new division of the Post Office offering facilities management, manufacturing and consulting services known as RoMEC (Royal Mail Engineering Consultancy). Initially a light grey livery (Seagull grey) was adopted and the existing fleet quickly repainted into the new colours, but in 1991, white replaced grey as the base colour.

Illustrating the Welsh version of the seagull grey RoMEC livery is Ford Transit E468PKG (6510015), pictured at Cross Keys in July 1990. In recent years, the bilingual lettering has been dropped and RoMEC vans in Wales carry the standard letters though now displayed as a single word. *D A Cott*

Not all engineering vans are operated by Romec. This photograph illustrates an LDV Sherpa M379TYG (3510011) in Royal Mail livery at Sheffield in May 1999. *M W Skillen*

Illustrating the Post Office Engineering identity used before RoMEC was created, this Ford Escort G576VRG (9520001) is pictured at Sunderland in October 1990. *D A Cott*

The last batch of Ford Escorts for Romec, delivered in 2001-02, adopted a new identity dropping the former abbreviation RoMEC for the word Romec as the company name and adding a red swirl on the bodywork. Earlier vans have received this revised identity as illustrated by T380KAR (8520153) used by a mobile cleaner was photographed at Hull in July 2005. Note that the earler lettering style has been retained on the bonnet. *D Longbottom*

In November 2000, the Post Office announced that it was seeking a joint venture partner for the RoMEC business that was rebranded as 'Romec' to make it more attractive to potential partners. In September 2002, Consignia selected Haden Building Management, a subsidiary of Balfour Beatty, and signed contracts for the joint venture. The Royal Mail Group retains a 51% stake in the joint venture. The existing fleet was transferred and continues to be maintained by Royal Mail in its workshops.

Type code 51 was used in 1986 for a batch of Ford Transit 16 cwt. vans; previously, postal engineering vans of this size but with petrol engines had been coded 54. 1987 saw the order be awarded to Freight-Rover for sixty-four Sherpas and orders were divided between the two types until 1996 when the LDV Pilot was the exclusive choice for the next five years. The 2005 delivery was for twenty Ford Transit T260 swb vans.

Type code 52 was also used in 1986, this time for the Ford Escort 1.6 diesel van. Annual deliveries have continued with a final order for two hundred and twenty-one Ford Escort 75s delivered early in 2002. A batch of seventy-eight Vauxhall Combos was delivered early in 2005.

Type code 53 was used for the small postal engineering vans with petrol engines up to 1985. The Bedford HA was bought up to 1981. The 1982-1983 deliveries were British Leyland Itals and the 1984 order was a mixture of Ford Escorts 4530001-30 and Austin Maestros 4530031-66. A further sixty-three Maestros were bought in 1985.

The Mailvan Handbook

Types 54 to 59

Type code 54 was used for postal engineering vans of 15/16 cwt capacity with petrol engines. Between 1970 and 1981, Commer and later Dodge Spacevans similar in specification to those bought or leased for Post Office Telephones were obtained for postal engineering duties. In the 1983-85 period, a mixture of Ford Transit 120s and Freight-Rover Sherpa K2s were bought for this work. Thereafter diesel engines were specified coded 51.

Type code 55 was allocated to larger vehicles used for postal engineering, mainly one-offs such as stores vans including a batch of eight Ford A stores vans with Cheshire Fire Engineering bodywork bought in 1981. More recently batches of LDV Convoys with low roofs, 7550001-30 in 1997, 8550001-11 in 1998, 4550001-15 in 2005 have joined the RoMEC fleet.

Vauxhall Combos were chosen for a batch of 78 vans for Romec delivered early in 2005. The white livery was retained but it included a colourful blue panel with the red Romec lettering superimposed on a blue map of the British Isles. The various facilities provided by the joint venture are listed on the back of the van. ET54LDZ (4520069) was pictured in Hull in June 2005. *D Longbottom*

In addition to the Vauxhall Combos, Ford Transit vans, LDV Convoy vans and LDV Convoy dropside trucks were added to the Romec fleet in 2005. Illustrated is one of four Convoy lwb vans with the standard LDV high-roof and used on pillarbox maintenance duties, BX05HMF (4580002), at the Warwick Romec depot in June 2005. *C M Hogan*

Type code 56 was allocated in 1971 to estate cars used for postal engineering duties or television detection duties. Two BL Ital 1.3 estate cars, 3560001/2, were bought in 1982. More recently, Leyland-DAF 45.130s with bodywork similar to 740cf mailvans joined the RoMEC fleet numbered 7560001-3.

Type code 57 was allocated in 1971 to postal engineering trailers. Over the years, this code has been used for a handful of trailers used for carriage of lpg bottles, pillar-box installation and general engineering purposes.

Type code 58 was allocated to larger stores van and trucks. Delivered in 1982 were two Leyland Boxer 12-ton stores truck with Aitken of Linlithgow bodywork and an Atlas hoist. The code was used again in 2005 on a delivery of four LDV Convoy high-roof vans for Romec.

Finally type code 59 remained vacant until it was used in 1984 for two Douglas Tugmaster shunters. Two LDV Convoy extra long-wheelbase dropside trucks for Romec numbered 4590001/2 were delivered in 2005.

Type 60

Type code 60 was introduced in 1987 for a higher-capacity version of the 7.5 tonne van. The body was lengthened to 4.88m and widened to 2.5m giving a capacity of 850cf. The first were eighty Ford Cargo 0813 vehicles with a mixture of Papworth and Besco bodywork numbered 7600001-80 with a further hundred similar vehicles following in 1988. 1989 saw a switch to the Leyland Roadrunner 8.13 chassis with Besco bodywork and Ratcliff tail-lifts numbered 9605001-96 and 9607001-10, the latter for Network Two duties. A further one hundred and seventy-seven similar vehicles were supplied in 1990. 1991 saw a change to the Leyland-DAF 45.130 chassis with similar vehicles supplied in 1992 (35), 1994 (92), 1996 (153), 1998 (38), 2000 (159). The final delivery in 2001 was a batch of DAF LF45s with Cartwright bodywork serialled 1607001-95.

Rationalisation in Parcelforce Worldwide in 2002 considerably reduced the number of parcels vans. The 850cf vans, with their tail-lifts, were suitable for redeployment on Royal Mail duties and many redundant 850cfs from the 2000 and 2001 batches were relettered for Royal Mail.

Royal Mail tried Ford Cargos with longer and wider bodies rated at 850cf in 1987. D421TTM (7600002) with Penman bodywork is seen at Warrington in October 1987. Registration of this batch was unusually undertaken by Ford before delivery. Full-width bodies were found to be a problem in many locations and most subsequent deliveries for mail duties had narrower 2.2 metre wide bodies rated at 740cf. *P Eckersley*

Leyland Roadrunner 850cf J828DRB (0605177) is shown at Norwich in July 1994. It carries the first version of the Parcelforce livery with embossed cyphers on the cab doors and gold Royal Mail lettering, both later deleted from the livery. *D A Cott*

One other use of this code was in 1991 by Royal Mail when a single Leyland-DAF 7.5 chassis-cab fitted with a demountable mobile kitchen body for use by Quadrant, the Post Office catering organisation, was given serial number 1600001.

Type 61

Type code 61 was introduced in 1987 for the Royal Mail variant of the larger 7.5 tonne van. Body length was again 4.88m but body-width remained at 2.21m, giving a capacity of 740cf.

Initially both 600cf and 740cf mailvans were bought together but after 1991, the 740cf became the standard 7.5 tonner on Royal Mail duties. The 1987 order was for 134 Leyland Roadrunner chassis fitted with Locomotors, Papworth or Tidd bodywork. The 1988 order was divided between 8610001-104 on Iveco Cargo 0813 chassis with Boalloy, Locomotors or Tidd bodywork and six more Leyland Roadrunners with Tidd bodywork. The 1989 order included thirty-nine Leylands fitted with bodywork built by the Post Office at Bamber Bridge and Kidbrooke,

The Mailvan Handbook

The Ford Cargo chassis gained a share of Royal Mail's orders in 1988 and an Iveco prefix in 1989. H81FNK (0610133L) is pictured at Seascale in September 1993. *P Eckersley*

together with fifty-six more with Tidd bodywork and eighty-three Cargos with Bamber Bridge bodywork. The 1991 delivery was exclusively Cargos and the delivery of 137 included 116 with Bamber Bridge bodywork. Another ninety-three Bamber Bridge bodied Cargos arrived in 1991, together with three of the new Leyland-DAF 45 model for evaluation. As a result two hundred and one of the new Leyland-DAF model followed. Iveco had also updated its Cargo and the new model, the Cargo 75E14, with its four-cylinder engine, proved to be problematic with Royal Mail. So the bodies were rechassised under warranty with new Cargo 75E15 chassis with six-cylinder engines.

The 1993 order was for one hundred and fifty more Cargos (ten of which were later rechassised) and two hundred and eighty more Leyland-DAF 45s with Cartwright, Tidd or Vaile bodywork. The repair depot at Bamber Bridge had closed in favour of a more compact location at an industrial unit at Chorley and it won the order for the bodies on Leyland-DAFs 3610301-30. Fords having disgraced itself as a supplier, the 1994 order was made up of 469 Leyland-DAF 45.130s and fifteen MAN 8-153s with Boalloy Tautliner, Chorley, Marshall and Vaile bodywork. 1995 orders were for a further one hundred and four Leyland-DAF 45.130s with Marshall bodywork followed by three hundred and seventy similar vans in 1996.

1997 deliveries were for twenty-seven MANs and 164 Leyland-DAF 45s all equipped with tail-lifts. Previous deliveries had featured a proportion of vehicles without tail-lifts and there was a programme in the late-1990s to retrofit tail-lifts to those 740cf vehicles without them. The reason was the increasing use of the new York trolley for mail transit rather than the humble mailbag.

The 1998 delivery was made up of thirty-six MANs and 334 Leyland-DAF 45.130s with Boalloy or Marshall bodywork. The 1999 order for 295 vans was similar with twenty-nine MANs and 266 Leyland-DAFs, one of which featured Cartwright curtain-sided bodywork. The 2000 order was for 577 vans, thirty-seven MANs and 540 DAFs, including a pre-production prototype of the new LF45 chassis. Fords returned to favour in the 2001 order for 448 vans, with 114 Cargo 75E17s among 334 DAF LF45s. A batch of the DAFs (1612001-92) had the wider 2.5m 850cf bodywork for use on Central London Distribution duties.

The availability of redundant Parcelforce Worldwide 850cf vans plus the move by Royal Mail towards larger vans and motive units for trunking duties had reduced recent orders to twenty-four DAF LF45s and six Iveco Cargo Tectors 75E15s in 2002 and to 169 DAFs and Ivecos in 2003. 2004 deliveries were exclusively DAF LF45 with Cartwright bodywork, featuring a mixture of Ratcliff, RSG and Dhollandia tail-lifts and a small batch with roller-bed floors for container transfer to and from airports. The bulk of the 2005 order was also for the same combination, but a small batch of twenty-five of Avia D75-150 chassis-cabs with Derek Jones Bodywork (both new suppliers for Royal Mail) were supplied in October 2005.

After the problems with the Cargos, the Leyland-DAF 45 was the exclusive choice in the mid-1990s, later to be joined by some MANs. Leyland-DAF 45.130 740cf L745GFC (2610286) with Tidd bodywork was photographed at Edinburgh in August 1998. Note the RAILNET 6 sticker in the windscreen; Railnet was the code name for the network of rail services based on mail distribution centres such as the Princess Royal centre at Willesden that ceased in 2003/4. *M D Street*

The later Cargo introduced in 1992 was less successful on Royal Mail duties and some were re-chassised with six-cylinder engines. Iveco-Ford Cargo with Vaile 740cf bodywork, L748GNM (3610124), is seen at Manchester. *M D Street*

The current standard 740cf mailvan is the DAF LF45 with Cartwright bodywork. MV05GVA (5610455) is pictured newly in service in the Haymarket in central London in August 2005. It is based at the South London mail centre at Nine Elms. *D Longbottom*

Type 62

The first use of type code 62 was in 1974 on a small, short-lived, batch of Vespa 'Vespino' 49cc mopeds bought in 1974. The code was then reissued in 1987 on a batch of 152 mailvans rated at 430cf/450cf capacity. They were a mixed batch with Iveco Daily 49.10 panel vans fitted out by Papworth with a high-roof numbered 7620001-16, Mercedes-Benz 609D vans 7620017-26, and Renault S56 panel vans 7620027-31. The remaining one hundred and twenty-one were chassis-cabs with separate bodywork made up of 7620032-41, Renault S56s with Bedwas bodies, 7620042-51, Mercedes-Benz 609Ds also with Bedwas bodywork and 7620052-152, Iveco Daily with Brade-Leigh bodywork. 1988 saw the arrival of a further one hundred and forty-six Iveco Dailys with Brade-Leigh bodywork plus seventeen more Mercedes with Papworth bodywork. Just nine more Iveco Dailys, 9620001-9, but with Saxon bodywork, were bought in 1989.

Meanwhile, Parcelforce had also identified a need for a vehicle intermediate to its 380cf Sherpa and 850cf 7.5 tonner. A single Volkswagen LT50 with Vaile box body, 8625001, arrived in 1988 and a further sixty were supplied in 1989. Also supplied to Parcelforce in 1989 were twenty-six Iveco Daily 49.10 Luton vans and twenty-four Iveco Turbo Zeta 79.12 panel vans. A final batch of thirty-six Iveco Daily 49.12 for Parcelforce was bought in 1992, and thereafter requirements for this size of van were met with the 530cf parcels van (type code 18).

One of the small batch of distinctive Volkswagen LT50 parcel vans bought in 1989, G998MFR (9627060) was photographed in Manchester in April 1992. *P Eckersley*

The 550cf mailvan was introduced in 1993 for the carriage of York containers in the provinces and mails in central London. Renault B120-65 M538LYL (3620150) contrasts with Iveco Daily 59.13 M844AUG (4620040) at Sheffield in May 1999. *M W Skillen*

Royal Mail bought a single Volkswagen LT50 mailvan, 1620001, in 1992. The following year, Royal Mail updated the design and the capacity to 550cf. The body was extended to 3.33m, allowing ten York trolleys to be accommodated within the body and within the six tonnes gvw of the vehicles. A total of one-hundred and two 550cf vehicles was supplied, the majority mounted on the Iveco Turbo Daily 59.12 with ten on the Renault B110-60 chassis. All featured the lightweight vertical descent folding platform tail-lift. In 1993, 90 Iveco Dailys and 65 of the slightly higher capacity Renault B120-65 operating at 6.5tonnes gvw arrived. One of the Renaults, 3620153, was fitted with a curtain-sided flatbed body with an extended rear platform for use at Edinburgh Airport. The platform was built by the Post Office at Chorley. Loose mailbags are unloaded onto the platform and are then driven to the terminal at the airport.

Sixty-five more were bought in 1994 (fifteen Renault and fifty Iveco) and seventy in 1995 (fifteen Renault and fifty-five Iveco). The Renault cab was unpopular with drivers, particularly when frequent stops were to be made, because it was much higher than the Iveco cabs. From 1996, the orders were solely for Iveco with twenty-five in 1996, 24 in 1997, 68 (including one lpg powered) in 1998, and 101 in 1999. The heavier Daily 64.12 was specified for the first batch bought in 2000 totalling 93 and a second batch on the updated Daily 65C15 followed numbered 0621001-38. Sixty similar vans came in 2001, 12 in 2002, 56 in 2003 and 23 in 2004.

Types 63 to 66

Type codes 62-70 were originally intended for vehicles used on, or in connection with, the delivery of telegrams. Code 63 was allocated for Puch MV50 mopeds bought for use on telegram delivery between 1972 and 1979. When telegram delivery ceased in October 1982, some survivors found further use on mail deliveries. Code 65 was allocated to the BSA Bantam motor-cycles used on telegram delivery. The use of BSA machines on mail and telegram duties can be traced back to 1921 and included some of the earliest motor cycle combinations (with side carriers).

Type code 64 was used for two Leyland Roadrunner 6-12 chassis cabs, 7640001/2, bought in 1987 by Parcelforce followed by five more the following year. These operated with demountable 850cf bodies 7650001-4 and 8655001-10. Another six Besco bodies, this time of 1400cf were bought in 1989 for use with 9687001 followed by a further sixteen in 1990 for use with skeletal trailers 0665001-5.

The original use of type code 66 was on Raleigh mopeds used on telegram deliveries. It was used again in 1984 on two batches of moped used on mail delivery work - BSA ER1M mopeds 4660001-35 and Tomos A3M mopeds 4660201-35. In 1985, the Post Office bought BSA Easyrider ER1K mopeds 5660036-85, Tomos A3MS 5660236-71 and Honda City Express mopeds 5660401-30. The Honda City Express was adopted as the standard machine with forty-five in 1987 with similar deliveries annually through to 2001. Thereafter just five were delivered in 2002 and a solitary machine in 2003.

Illustrated is the first of a batch of 35 BSA Easyrider ER1M mopeds bought in 1984, C301ANB (4660001), at Bolton in March 1987. The modern BSAs were no match for Japanese competition and the Honda City Express became the standard moped from 1987.
P. Eckersley

Types 67 to 69

Type code 67 was initially allocated to vans used on telegram delivery work, when BLMC Minivans were bought specifically for this work between 1976 and 1981.

Parcelforce used the code in 1987 for two ERFs with Locomotors bodywork while an ERF 900cf van was supplied in 1989 numbered 9677001. Royal Mail used code 67 for the Honda Foreman S TRX450 quadbike 1670001 bought in February 2002 for use on the island of Kerrera. Being a private island off Oban, Kerrera does not require the machine to be licensed, and the problem of only being able to license a quadbike as an agricultural vehicle did not apply.

The only use of type code 68 until 2005 was on a drawbar trailer bought in 1987 and on a similar trailer in 1989, both used with ERF vehicles with code 67. Two Honda Dylan SES 125cc motorcycles numbered 4680001/2 were supplied in January 2005 for use in central London on *Sameday* deliveries.

Type code 69 was allocated in 1987 for the diesel-engined Ford Escort mailcar. Eighty Ford Escort 1.6L diesel mailcars were bought in 1987, followed by a further two in 1991. Parcelforce used code 69 for a batch of seven similar Ford Escorts in 1988.

Unregistered Honda Foreman quadbike 1670001 at Kerrera Pier in August 2002. *D A Cott*

Type 70

This code has been used for Sherpa and Convoy 3.2m long-wheelbase high-roof vans of 380cf and 400cf capacity. The first two, 5700001/2, were supplied in 1985 and large batches have been supplied each year for use by Royal Mail. The standard version has a nearside door, rear shutters and the extra high Post Office roof and the same changes of manufacturer and model have applied to these vans as detailed for the 320cf van (type code 14). Two vans, 5700218/9, were bought in 1995 with rear tail-lift stowed under the rear of vehicle; they have the standard Hiloader high roof rather than the Post Office extra high roof. The 400cf can carry four York trolleys. From 1996, rear slam doors and the standard Hiloader roof has been an option on these vans. Another twenty-nine Ratcliff tail-lift fitted Convoys 400cfs were bought in 2000.

Two other vehicles for Royal Mail duties with this type code are 3703000, a Leyland-DAF 400 chassis-cab fitted with a Post Office lightweight body built at Kidbrooke with a rear tail-lift, designed for the transport of York trolleys.

Illustrating the early Freight-Rover badged 400cf mailvan with the special Post Office extra-high-roof is D868LKP (6700130). *M W Skillen*

In contrast, the standard Parcelforce Sherpa had the standard Leyland-DAF high-roof that was lower than the special Royal Mail version and this is evident in this view of H655BSP (0705460) photographed in May 1991 in Dundee. The embossed cyphers were quickly dropped and replaced by a standard transfer. *D M Hinde*

The LDV Convoy mailvan with the special Post Office high roof is a familiar sight in large cities on box collections and bulk deliveries, none more so than in London. R614WOB (7700295) based at London's South East Delivery Office was photographed on Waterloo Road in March 1999. *D Longbottom*

Parcelforce Worldwide has in recent years franchised out a proportion of its delivery operation to self-employed drivers with their own vans. The vehicles carry the standard Parcelforce Worldwide lettering on what presumably should be standard Post Office Service Red but sometimes the colour is maroon or even orange as illustrated in this view taken in Stourbridge. The long-wheelbase Mercedes-Benz Sprinter has been a popular choice for these vehicles but other types include Fords, Renaults and LDVs. *C M Hogan*

It was trialled extensively at Tonbridge, Sheffield, Guildford, King's Lynn and Diss but no further vans were bought and the tail-lift fitted 400cf described above is used instead. Secondly, Mercedes-Benz supplied a Sprinter van with a tail-lift in 1996 for evaluation and this was given serial 6701000.

One other van worthy of special mention is 2700000, a green Concept vehicle bought in 1992 with a number of environmentally-friendly features including engine noise reduction kit, composite road springs, asbestos-free brake lining, Telma retarder, catalytic exhaust and spray suppression kit. It was finished in green livery and it operated at Southampton.

The 1994 and 1997 deliveries including a number finished in Quadrant's white livery for use as catering vans including a number with refrigeration units. Quadrant was restructured as a joint venture, initially with Granada and now with the Compass Group, and vehicles are no longer procured through Royal Mail.

Parcelforce also used this size of vehicle extensively and they are a familiar sight delivering parcels. The first batch was 108 Freight-Rover Sherpa 300s bought in 1986; they differed from the Royal Mail version in having the standard Hiloader high-roof and rear unglazed slam doors and as a result, they were classified as 380cf. Large batches were supplied

The Mailvan Handbook

annually from 1986 to 1994 and from 1998 to 2001 but in the interim the Iveco Daily was favoured. The Parcelforce Worldwide reorganisation significantly reduced the requirement for 380cf vans and many Convoys were either sold prematurely, given Royal Mail lettering and used on letter duties or repainted white for use by the Logistics arm on internal mail contracts.

Deliveries of the first order from Royal Mail for the new LDV Maxus were beginning in October 2005 as this Handbook was being finalised.

This view shows BX54MRY (4700291), based at Mount Pleasant in London, at nearby Ludgate Hill in May 2005. This van contrasts with the earlier Convoy in being fitted with the standard LDV roof and rear slam doors. Bought in increasing numbers including, in some cases, being fitted with rear tail-lifts for the carriage of York containers to and from smaller offices.
D Longbottom

After a £500m five-year development programme, LDV announced its new Maxus van in January 2005 which will replace its Convoy van. Royal Mail is one of LDV's biggest customers and a total of six demonstrators were supplied. A further four demonstrators of the Maxus 3.2/95 model with extra-high roof and rear slam doors entered service at Southwark delivery office in September 2005. BU05OUN (5700345) was photographed leaving the South London mail centre.
F J Weston

Types 71 and 72

Type code 71 was allocated in 1986 to a small batch of one hundred Austin Maestro 80cf mailvans fitted with diesel engines (see type code 88 for the petrol-engined variant). They proved to be much noisier in service than the standard Ford Escorts and several were relegated to postal engineering and other duties. Three more arrived in 1989 but Royal Mail did not buy the Maestro again.

Type codes 72 to 74 are allocated to cars. The division between the three types is on the basis of engine capacity; code 72 is for cars of up to 1800cc, 73 for cars between 1800cc and 2000cc and 74 for cars with an engine capacity of more than two litres. There is no distinction made in the coding between petrol and diesel engined vehicles.

There is a tendency for one manufacturer to provide the majority of cars in a given year as follows: 1982, Vauxhall had the majority of orders with its Chevette, Ford Escorts dominated in 1983 and 1984, the Austin Montego was bought in 1985 while the Ford Escort was in favour from 1986 to 1989 followed by Peugeot in 1990 and 1991.

The move towards diesel-engined cars with their larger engines has meant the majority of cars recently have been coded 73.

Since 2001, policy appears to favour the used of small crewbuses (Peugeot Partners and Renault Kangoos) and the type is considered suited to many postbus duties. Here is one of the latest arrivals lettered for Postbus duties.

Austin supplied Maestros in both 1984 and 1986 but thereafter lost out to Ford with its Escort for the bulk of Royal Mail's requirements. Illustrated here, Austin Maestro diesel mailvan D517SDT (6710099) was pictured in Chesterfield during April 1991. *D J Foster*

Ford Escort saloon E964BJA (7720061) was photographed at Bolton in August 1988. The application of full 'Royal Mail' lettering to the doors was unusual and most remained indistinguishable from private vehicles. *P Eckersley*

Types 73 and 74

Type code 73 was used in small numbers until 1987 when a larger delivery of Fords (Sierras and Granadas) was supplied. Between 1988 and 2001, the years' deliveries were a mixture of Peugeots and Fords of different types, mainly with diesel engines. The majority of cars are not lettered although many are finished in the manufacturer's standard red. Several have found use as postbuses, some permanently, others when the regular bus or estate car is not available.

In 2002, the type code 73 was used for two batches of 4-seat crewbuses in full Royal Mail livery comprising Renault Kangoos 2730001-14 and Peugeot Partners 2730015-94. These two batches are similar to the standard crewbuses (type code 89) but appear to have been allocated as replacements for cars on Royal Mail duties.

Type code 74 is used for large cars and Fords, Rovers and Jaguars have been bought in small numbers for use by directors and senior managers.

Escort estate car M462UWR (4734011) spent most of its service in Chesterfield but ended its days with the Post Office as a Christmas extra at York in December 1998. It was photographed at the York overflow parking area, overlooking York station, at the end of December that year. *D Longbottom*

Peugeot 306 car V436DLM (9730456) is unusual for a pool car in having the Royal Mail cruciform on the front doors – usually such cars are just plain red. New as a Leeds based vehicle, it went to Driffield in January 2000 where it spent a long time on the Driffield-Skipsea postbus route, after the withdrawal of a Ford Mondeo estate car. It was photographed at Skipsea Sands, overlooking Bridlington Bay, in January 2000. *D Longbottom*

Six of the four-seat crewbuses delivered in 2002/3 were used as postbuses. One of the Renault Kangoos, HV52YNG (2730002), new to Peterborough as a pool car, was declared surplus after seven months use and it was redeployed to Morpeth where it has become the regular bus on the Netherwitton service. The only change is the addition of the Post Bus and associated legal lettering. *D Longbottom*

Types 75 and 76

Type codes 75 to 77 are allocated to postbuses. These have been covered in detail in the sister publication The Postbus Handbook and this book will only cover recent purchases.

The 1998 order for postbuses was made up of LDV Pilot 9-seaters 8750001-16, 8750021-4 and 8750028/9 plus LDV Convoy 14-seaters 8750017-20 and 8750025-7. The 1999 order was a small one for 9750001, Pilot and 9750002-5, Convoys. The interior layout of the Pilots was considered unsatisfactory and 9750001 was used at St. Albans as a standard crewbus with the security grill removed and no further Pilot postbuses were bought by Royal Mail. LDV constructed a flat-roof Convoy in the spring of 1998 as an alternative and this vehicle, R783AOE, was taken on demonstration on various routes in Scotland; it was bought by Royal Mail in March 2000 and given serial 8750100, and it worked at Morpeth.

The 2000 delivery was for ten standard Convoys numbred 0750001-10 followed by seven more in 2001 (1750001-7). In 2002, the numerous postbuses bought in 1996 were nearing the end of their lives, requiring a replacement for the LDV Pilot as the smaller postbus.

Y47TJW (0750004) at Ayr workshop in August 2001, where it had been stored for a number of months prior to entering service as Brodick-BK10. The delay was due to it having 15 seats, more than any of the Arran drivers were licensed to drive and eventually the expedient decision was taken to downseat it to carry seven.
D A Cott

LDV Convoy 14-seat postbus BU05KFO (5753004) turns at Littlebury for return to its Saffron Walden base. It is seen on the early afternoon run of the Langley/Littlebury-Saffron Walden service in August 2005, its third day in service. *D A Cott*

Peugeot 406 postbus Y594RBY (0760030) was photographed at Oban in May 2001, while it was a reserve between March 2001 and June 2003, moving to the Aros-Ulva Ferry postbus route. This estate car was scheduled to be replaced at Aros by Vauxhall Combo postbus 5760007 in November 2005. *D A Cott*

The low-roof LDV Convoy was introduced in 2003 as a replacement for the LDV Pilot on postbus duties. Two types have been obtained – a 10-seat version with glazed rear doors and an 8-seat version with solid rear doors and a rear mail compartment. Both types have a front mailbox in the cab next to the driver. Illustrating the more numerous 8-seaters is BU05KFD (5751002) from the 2005 delivery. It is seen leaving Stafford delivery office in August 2005 before taking up service on the Eccleshall route. *D Longbottom*

A single standard Convoy was bought numbered 2750101 (a further three were cancelled) and an experimental Convoy with flat roof, eight seats, a full-height mail cage at the back and unglazed rear windows was bought numbered 2750105 and placed in service at Builth Wells. A single Mercedes-Benz Vario O814 with Frank Guy 22-seat bodywork (3755001) arrived for use at Coton House, but was rejected as unsuitable.

Further similar Convoys were bought in 2003-04 to replace the 1996 delivery of Pilots and Convoys as follows: forty-one Convoys similar to 2750105 numbered 3751001-41; 3752001-12, flat roof Convoys seating ten without the rear mail cages and twenty high-roof Convoys seating fourteen numbered 3753001-20. None were required in 2004 while 2005 deliveries were at the time of writing 5751001-3, 5752001 and 5753001-6.

Type code 76 is used for estate cars used as postbuses. 1998 saw the arrival of fifteen Peugeot 406LXDT estate cars number 8760001-15, followed by similar 9760001 in 1999, 0760001-30 in 2000 and 1760001-8 in 2001. Since 2001, policy appears to favour the used of small crewbuses (Peugeot Partners and Renault Kangoos with codes 73 or 89) on these duties. The type is considered suited to many postbus duties with separate passenger doors and rear mail compartment. The first batch, 5760001-13, were Vauxhall Combos, specifically bought for postbus duties, were due in November 2005 and would start to replace the Peugeot 406s of 2000.

The Mailvan Handbook

Types 77 and 78

Type code 77 was allocated in 1980 for Land Rover postbuses. In 1987, 1991 and 1997, Land Rover mailvans, proper to code 10, were given type code 77. Vehicle 5770001, from 1995, was a Land Rover Defender 110 postbus bought in 1995.

Type code 78 was similarly allocated to crewbuses in 1980. The Post Office had a limited requirement for vehicles moving staff between locations but the tendency to relocate city centre sorting offices to industrial parks on the outskirts brought an increased requirement for staff transport. Ford Transit 12-seat crewbuses were bought in 1981 (15), 1983 (22), 1984 (8) and 1985 (14) for such duties together with two Freight-Rover Sherpa 310 14-seaters in 1984.

1987 saw the arrival of 34 Freight-Rover Sherpa 12-seaters and these were used to take postmen from their delivery office to their point of delivery quickly and hence accelerate the start of their deliveries. A further 161 followed in 1988 and 72 in 1989. Deliveries continued through the 1990s, predominately with the smaller Leyland-DAF 200s with 105 in 1990, 282 in 1991, 36 in 1992, and 293 in 1993. The larger Leyland-DAF 400 was also specified with 39 bought in 1990, 28 in 1991 and four in 1992.

Land Rover 60cf mailvan R224JSG (7770006) at Alford in July 2001. *D A Cott*

Ford Transit minibuses were bought between 1981 and 1985 for crewbus duties and C515 EHG (5780005) from the 1985 delivery is pictured in Blackburn in June 1988. *P Eckersley*

Freight-Rover Sherpas crewbuses and their successors have been obtained by Royal Mail in large numbers from 1987 to date, and are used extensively by most delivery offices to speed postmen to the start of their delivery rounds. A rather battered and faded Leyland-DAF 400 crewbus L617EPG (3780343) was photographed at Havant. New with 14 seats, it appears to have lost the rearmost seats, judging by the wire mesh on the windows. It was sold by the Post Office a year after this photograph was taken in September 1997. *D Longbottom*

Leyland-DAF 200 crewbus L897OGW (3780291) in Eastbourne in September 1997. Note the Brighton lettering below the cypher – this was carried by some vehicles in the South East in the 1990s and was reminiscent of the allocation lettering carried on mailvans in GPO days. *D Longbottom*

Royal Mail found that the fully-seated bus was too restrictive - waiting for all twelve postmen to complete sorting their walks inevitably meant that at least one would get delayed for one reason or another, affecting the other eleven. Another problem was that fully-seated crewbuses could not accommodate second and third sacks of mail that postmen frequently had to deliver, as mail volumes continued to increase. To overcome these problems, a multi-purpose Leyland-DAF 400 was developed in 1993. The layout included six seats in the front (two next to the driver, four in a row immediately behind the cab) with a multi-purpose rear loadspace separately by a threequarter width mesh partition from the front able to provide stowage for sacks of mail, up to six bicycles or eight postmen on twin longitudinal seating in the rear. Twenty-three of this type were delivered in 1993.

An eight-seat version was introduced in 1994 on the LDV 200 crewbus with two rows of seats behind the cab and a rear loadspace with solid rear doors. There was a similar nine-seat LDV 400 crewbus with the same general layout. However, these types were unable to carry bicycles.

From 1995, the LDV 400 multi-purpose carrier had the longitudinal seating and the rear window deleted from the specification, so that there

LDV Pilot 5-seat crewbus with rear mail compartment Y636BOA (1780057) at Ayr workshop in August 2001. Since 2003, this type has been coded 91. *D A Cott*

Romec provides a service between Chesterfield station and the various Royal Mail Group offices in Chesterfield as part of its facilities management contract. Not a real postbus, LDV Pilot V950LOA (9780122) was new to Royal Mail at Cheltenham, but was repainted white and transferred to Chesterfield, where it was photographed in February 2004. *D J Foster*

LDV Convoy multi-purpose vehicle R177BOC (8780181) at York in December 1998. In addition to the carriage of postmen and mail, these buses can also carry up to six bicycles in the rear compartment. In 2003, this type was given code 92. *D Longbottom*

was only one window behind the cab section. Also introduced in 1995 was the comparable LDV 200 crewbus with five passenger seats (two next to the driver and three in a row behind), with a full height and width glazed partition between passenger accommodation and the rear loadspace. Again there was no window in the rear section or the rear doors, nor was the type able to carry bicycles.

1996 saw the change from LDV 200 to LDV Pilot and from LDV 400 to LDV Convoy. One other alteration was that some Convoys were specified with rear shutters (rather than rear slam doors) in common with the Convoy 400cf mailvan. Pilots and Convoys were each supplied in the three basic options (fully-seated, two rows of seats plus loadspace and one row of seats plus larger loadspace) between 1997 and 2002, although the numbers of fully-seated crewbuses bought was increasingly limited.

Type code 78 has not been used for new vehicles since 2003, with new full-seated crewbuses having type code 79; LDV Pilots with five seats and rear mail compartment having type code 91 and diesel LDV Convoys with six seats and a rear mail compartment having type code 92.

Types 79 and 80

Type code 79 was issued in 1980 for fuel bowsers and fuel tankers. By 2003, the code had become vacant and it was decided to rationalise the various types of crewbus and provide separate codes for the main types. Code 79 was chosen for the Convoy crewbus with 209 supplied in 2003 and 8 in 2004 made up of flat roof 8-seaters with rear loadspace, high-roof 9-seaters with rear loadspace and some high-roof 11-seater crewbuses.

Type code 80 has been used since 1971 for workshop vehicles. A network of one hundred and twenty Vehicle Services workshops looks after Royal Mail's fleet of cars, vans and trucks. To do this, workshops are allocated two fleets of vehicles, a small number of reserve vans of the common types to substitute for vehicles being serviced and a number of workshop vans, mobile workshops, vans for fitters and some specialised recovery vehicles for use by the technicians themselves.

Code 80 is made up of a wide variety of vehicles. However, many vans used as workshop vans are standard mailvans retained for use as workshop vans at the end of their normal working lives. They retain the serial number allocated when new and hence are not coded 80.

Leyland-DAF 400 recovery vehicle L738PAV (3800209) at Diss in March 1994 with Ford Escort H81EPV (0871125) on the trailer. The current practice is not to buy such vehicles new but to convert time-expired Convoy mailvans or parcels vans instead. *D A Cott*

For more than twenty years, this 1981 Bedford TK1630 Recovery Vehicle was used by the Post Office to rescue vehicles in the West Midlands. Fitted with Crane Fruehauf bodywork and a Holmes Wrecker crane, it was initially operated on trade plates from the main Birmingham office in Royal Mail Street. Changes to the registration requirements led it to be registered E919TOL in January 1988 and it was refurbished in 1994 at Wolverhampton where it was photographed before return to Birmingham. *C Mattox*

Purpose-built workshop vans based on the Leyland-DAF 400 van were introduced in 1990 when eighteen were bought for use by Parcelforce, with a further twenty-four in 1990 (twenty for Royal Mail and four for Parcelforce). Another nine followed in 1992, four in 1993 and five in 1994. The equipment provided on the vans enabled technicians to deal with roadside breakdowns or to undertake maintenance and repairs at delivery offices without workshop facilities. Thus the vans have a compressed air supply, a generator to power electrical tools and a portable gas-welding pack as well as tools, spares and other equipment. In addition, a number of surplus 320cf mailvans were converted to workshop vans. No new workshop vans of this type have been bought since 1994, and the recent surplus of Parcelforce Convoy 380cf vans has partly been used by converting them for workshop duties.

To complement the mobile workshop vans, some trailers have been developed for workshop duties. One is the mobile workstation, a twin-axle trailer built at Chorley with a fully enclosed body with translucent roof to provide a sheltered working environment for vans of up to 150cf in size. Another trailer developed and built by the Post Office is the cycle trailer, a lightweight trailer able to carry up to eight cycles.

Vehicle recovery vehicles are again often redundant mailvans fitted with new bodies and the necessary equipment. A small number of recovery vehicles has been bought new including a Leyland-DAF 45.130 slideback recovery vehicle and an Iveco Turbo Daily 59.12 vehicle bought in 1992 with two more Leyland-DAFs, in 1994 and 1995.

Types 81 to 83

Types codes 81 to 83 were allocated in 1971 to the small fleet of mobile Post Offices with 82 allocated to the tenders and 83 to the trailers. These vehicles with their coachbuilt trailers provided a full postal service at shows and events. 1983 saw the purchase of the last traditional Mobile Post Office unit with the arrival of Ford Cargo 2115 motive unit 3810001 (diverted from the preceding year's delivery of 20/22-tonne artics) and Coventry Steel Caravans semi-trailer 3810002. Another semi-trailer followed in 1985 while two demountable Mobile Post Offices were delivered in 1992. These are thought to be emergency facilities rather than for traditional Mobile Post Office use.

While the traditional Mobile Post Office was no longer required, the Post Office developed a new type of Mobile Post Office for use in rural areas where the demand was insufficient to support a normal Post Office business. Two trial schemes have been introduced, one based at Carlisle serving rural locations in Cumbria and the other based at Tavistock serving locations each side of the Devon/Cornwall border. In time-honoured tradition, both schemes initially used life-expired vans, the Carlisle van being a 1989 Leyland Roadrunner 740cf mailvan, while the Tavistock scheme used a converted 1992 Sherpa from Parcelforce.

The replacement for the original Devon & Cornwall Mobile Post Office is this Vauxhall Movano 3500 van MF51YDB (1810001) new in February 2002 and pictured at Cargreen in August 2002. The counter area on this van is at the extreme rear of the van rather than on the nearside with shelter provided by the single rear hinged door. It is used three days a week in the Liskeard, Launceston and Tavistock areas. *C M Hogan*

Both of the Volkswagen Golf mailvans are visible in this view taken at Perth. L893LJB (5830001) is a Golf Ecomatic van while M984NBL (5830002) in the background has a conventional transmission. The Eco-Golf had an engine that automatically switched off when the vehicle was decelerating or was stationary, and started up again as soon as the throttle was pressed, reducing fuel consumption and pollution. It also had a semi-automatic gearbox with a gear lever but no clutch pedal. The trial was not extended to other vehicles.
P Walton

When replacement vehicles were needed, both schemes received new vans with Carlisle receiving an Iveco Daily lwb van converted by Papworth and numbered 0810001, while the replacement for the Tavistock vehicle was a Vauxhall Movano 3500. The vans are finished in Post Office Ltd's green livery with its 'lozenge' symbol and lettering. They operate to a fixed timetable with stops of 30-45 minutes at each location, generally served once a week.

The modern Mobile Post Office appears to be the solution to the problem of providing counter services in rural areas. A further three Mobile Post Offices, Fiat Ducatos with Torton bodywork, were supplied in summer 2005 and two have started new services in the Wick area in north-east Scotland and the Rhydlewis area of Ceredigion in west Wales.

The only recent use of type code 82 has been on a Tidd trailer 3820002 used for Public Relations duties and on two Renault Kangoos demonstrated to Royal Mail and later bought and given serials 0820001/2. The Renaults were notable in being finished in standard factory red, a much darker shade than the standard Post Office Service Red specified by Royal Mail.

Type 84

Type code 84 was allocated in 1971 to publicity caravans and display trailers. Its use has been extended over time to include all vehicles used on public relations work, vehicles preserved as publicity vehicles and other miscellaneous vehicles.

These vehicles included several full-sized buses and coaches bought secondhand by the Post Office as follows:

> 3840003, a former London Transport standard DMS, Leyland Fleetline FE30ALR, KJD5P, with MCW bodywork bought from Ensign in March 1984 and used as a exhibition unit entitled THE POST BUS.

> 5840001, another former London Transport Fleetline, KUC988P, also purchased from Ensign and used as an exhibition unit entitled WRITE IT.

> 5840002, a Bristol RELH6G bus, SVO95L, with Eastern Coach Works bodywork used as a mobile screening unit lettered MEDIBUS.

> 8840004, Leyland Leopard coach, OGT329P, with Plaxton coachwork used as a mobile medical centre lettered MEDIBUS.

> 8840005, a former London Transport Fleetline CRL6 bus, purchased from 3M(UK) in February 1989, KUC212P, was used as an exhibition unit lettered ROYAL MAIL ROADSHOW.

Vehicles bought new coded 84 include various cars, estate cars, Land Rovers, a Citroën C25 hot-air balloon retrieval vehicle and various trailers and semi-trailers.

Bristol RELH bus SVO95L (5840002) was converted to a mobile screening unit for the Post Office's Occupational Health Service. It is pictured at Diss workshop in November 1991 and was later sold to the London district of St John's Ambulance. The offside windows were overpanelled as part of the conversion.
D A Cott

The Post Office's Occupational Health Service operated a Leyland Leopard coach and a Bristol RELH6G for many years under the banner of Medibus. The Leyland Leopard coach with Plaxton coachwork was OGT329P (8840004). It was new to Epsom Coaches as a 51-seat coach and later passed to Hallen of Romford before being purchased by the Post Office in the late 1980s. It is pictured at Arley in May 1990. *D A Cott*

One of three former London Transport Fleetlines to join the Post Office fleet was KUC988P (5840001) converted to an exhibition unit promoting letter-writing entitled Write It. It was photographed at a Post Office event at the National Tramway Museum at Crich in Derbyshire in June 1989. *C M Hogan*

Types 85 and 86

Type code 85 was allocated in 1971 to television detectors, a function the Post Office continued to perform under contract to the BBC. The Post Office created a separate subsidiary Subscription Services Limited in October 1989.

A new fleet of television detector vans was bought in 1990/91 with twenty-two Leyland-DAF 400 lwb vans (9850001-14 and 0850001-8) in the familiar white and blue livery. In 1996/7, these were replaced with ten LDV 400s 6850001-10 (N633-642NAE) and ten LDV Convoys 7850001-10 (P226-30/6-40WWS). In April 1999, a new joint venture, Envision Licensing Limited, one-third owned by the Post Office and the remainder owned by Bull Holdings Limited and WPP Group Limited took over the contract with the BBC for television licensing. Envision ceased to trade after March 2001 and a new company, Consignia (Customer Management) Limited took over responsibility from April 2001. Consignia lost the contract for TV Licensing to Capita in July 2002. One other LDV Convoy minibus 1850001 (Y889BOA) was supplied in August 2001.

Type code 86 was allocated in 1983 to six Ford Transit 16-seat postbuses with a further similar vehicle delivered in 1984.

Leyland-DAF 400 television detector van H312BGY (0850008) was pictured at Thetford in May 1994. *D A Cott*

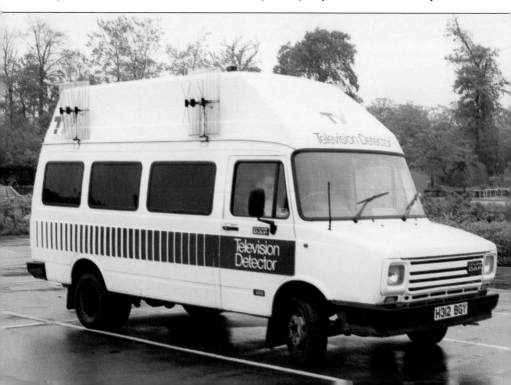

The last new Post Office Television Detector van was Y889BOA (1850001) delivered in August 2001 while the remaining nine of the order were cancelled. It was among those that passed to Capita, who took over this aspect of the buisness in July 2002. The van is still maintained by Royal Mail and is seen in 2005. *C M Hogan*

The first Ford Escort Mk IIIs were petrol engined. B787YFR (4890566) was photographed at Barbon PO, Kirkby Lonsdale in October 1986. *P Eckersley*

Type 87

Type code 87 was first allocated in 1984 to the diesel-engined Ford Escort van with a small batch of one hundred bought at the same time as a larger batch of petrol-engined Ford Escorts (type code 89). The Post Office decided to standardise on the diesel-engined version from 1985 and over fifty thousand Ford Escort mailvans had been supplied by Ford by the spring of 2002 when production ceased.

The Ford Escort was classified at 80cf capacity and was mainly used on collections and deliveries in towns and rural areas. Those bought as mailvans followed the various changes in production as Ford updated the model periodically.

The only year that the Ford Escort did not dominate deliveries was in 1992 when Royal Mail bought only one hundred and fifty Escorts, with the bulk of its order going to Vauxhall with its Astramax. The 1990 update to the Ford Escort was found to be unreliable and Vauxhall received the bulk of the 1992 order and much of that for 1993 with its Vauxhall Astramax. By 1994, the Escort was back in favour with the largest single delivery of 5,136 supplied in one contract year. However a second supplier of small mail vans continued to be a feature of the purchasing policy until 2001.

The normal life expectancy for a small mailvan in 1984 was five or six years but this had been reduced by the 1990s to about three years.

Ford updated the Escort to the Mk V version in 1991 and was rewarded with a large contract of 5,797 vans for Royal Mail and Quadrant duties. The most noticeable change was the slight raised-roof effect of the mail compartment of the body. Unfortunately for Ford, the updated version proved unsatisfactory in Royal Mail service and Vauxhall Astramaxes were bought in 1991 to 1993. From 1994 to 2001, the Ford Escort secured the lion's share of the Royal Mail small mailvan contract. Pictured here is H678MPR (1873952) at Dorchester in December 1994. *B C Read*

Illustrating both the final delivery of Ford Escorts in 2001-02 and the continuing use of local Northern Ireland registrations for most vehicles based in the province is MCZ2261 (1873051). New in February 2002, it is seen at its Newtownabbey base in August of that year. Vans in Northern Ireland carry the same livery as those in England. In total, some 50,019 Ford Escorts were supplied to Royal Mail for used as mailvans between 1984 and 2002, making the Ford Escort the most numerous mailvan and exceeding more than twofold the total Morris Minor mailvan purchases between 1953 and 1972 of 24,420. *C M Hogan*

Austin Maestro mailvan B379HUX (4880017) from the initial 1984 petrol-engined batch of seventy was photographed at Market Drayton in March 1986. *P Eckersley*

Type 88

The Post Office bought seventy petrol-engined Austin Maestro City mailvans in 1984 for evaluation against the Ford Escort, numbered 4880001-70. A further batch of Maestros, this time with diesel-engines (type code 71) was bought in 1986 but Austin was not successful in being awarded further orders and the Ford Escort reigned supreme until 1991.

The code was reissued in 1994 when one hundred Ford Courier Popular vans were bought for evaluation of the over-square design of small vans. The Vauxhall Combo was preferred for the type of vehicle and these were bought in reasonable numbers between 1994 and 2000.

Photographed at Tyldesley, is Ford Courier mailvan L816PBF (4880049). Although the type was limited to the initial order for one hundred vans, the Ford Courier was more successful in gaining orders from Royal Mail for the small four-seat crewbus version. *P Eckersley*

Type 89

As already noted, the initial use of type code 89 was on a batch of petrol-engined 80cf Ford Escort 35s, 4890001-1030, delivered in 1984.

The code was reissued in 1995 for small crewbuses with a capacity of driver and four postmen. They were used to overcome the problem of having all the postmen ready to commence their walks with a larger crewbus and also because the smaller crewbus could then be used on a rural delivery run in place of a standard 80cf van.

The first batch was for four hundred Ford Courier vans similar to those tried in 1994, except that the rear of the van had a row of three seats behind the cab, a moveable mesh partition to provide accommodation for mail or pouches, while a large single window was fitted on either side. Ford branded the type the Courier Kombi, but the staff christened them 'Popemobiles' on account of their large side windows. Further batches of three hundred and ninety one arrived in 1997, eight in 1998 and a final delivery of five hundred and eighty in 2000. In addition to their duties as crewbuses, several were used as postbuses on quieter routes.

The 2001 order was divided between the Peugeot Partner with 157 (1890001-156 and 1890209) and the Renault Kangoo (1870157-208) as was the 2002 order. The main 2003 order was for 683 Renault Kangoos plus three Vauxhall Combo crewbuses. A further three Combos were delivered in spring 2004 and all subsequent deliveries have been Combos.

Ford Courier Kombi N194LNW (5890030) has a routine service at Sheffield in May 1999. *M W Skillen*

A well-loaded HX53WFN (3890573), one of large batch of six hundred and eighty-three Renault Kangoo DCI8 4-seat crewbuses, obtained in 2003 seen here in its home town of Caernarfon in May 2005. The Partner, Kangoo and Combo all feature a separate passenger door on each side, making entry and exit much easier than on the earlier Ford Couriers. A two-year service life is planned for the Renault Kangoos with the first sales taking place in autumn 2005. The forthcoming Renault Kangoo 4x4 postbuses are expected to be similar to these vehicles, with raised 200mm ground clearance, 350mm wheels, deeper front and rear bumpers and Post Bus lettering. *D Longbottom*

The all-conquering Vauxhall Combo is Royal Mail's standard 4-seat crewbus, the monopoly being broken only by the small batch of Renault Kangoo 4x4s due in November 2005, as Vauxhall does not currently offer a Combo 4x4. Pictured is EN05GDO (5890369) at Kinross in August 2005. The solid panelling behind the passenger compartment allows the cruciform to be displayed on each side, making the identity of the operator much clearer than on the earlier Renault Kangoo. The forthcoming Combo postbuses are expected to be similar to these vehicles but with Post Bus lettering. *D A Cott*

Types 90 and 91

Type code 90 was allocated to diesel-engined Ford Fiesta vans in 1984 and a single batch of one hundred was bought in that year, following the purchase of petrol-engined Fiesta vans (type code 04) in 1983.

The only other use of this code has been as part of the current lpg experiment with ten 4-seat crewbuses included in the trial. Numbered 2902001-10, they are Peugeot Grant crewbuses similar to the Peugeot Partners.

Type code 91 was allocated in 1985 to the narrow, light 80cf mailvans when two Suzuki Super Carry vans were bought for use on the narrow roads on the Scilly Isles. Two Bedford Rascal vans were demonstrated in 1986 and two batches each of thirty-five followed in 1986 and 1987 and they were tried in rural areas where extremely narrow passageways were found. However, the Bedford Rascal with its 970cc petrol engine did not gain general acceptance and there were no further large orders apart from pairs of Rascals bought in 1988, 1990 and 1992. Royal Mail reverted to Suzuki in 1994 and 1997, when further pairs were bought for the Scilly Isles. Since then, standard mailvans have been used at St. Mary's with the current fleet being two Vauxhall Combos.

The first use of the narrow Bedford Rascal van for Royal Mail duties was on the Scilly Isles. Two small batches were then bought in both 1986 and 1987 for more widespread trials, including D376MDB (6910004) pictured at Northwich in April 1997. *P Eckersley*

Ford Fiestas were tried as both mailcars and mailvans during the 1983-1985 period. Pictured at Lairg during 1985, Ford Fiesta diesel mailvan B398TST (4900090) is hown here. The use of registration plates made up of individual plastic letters was a characteristic of Scottish mailvans during this period. *P Eckersley*

The current use of code 91 is on the LDV Pilot dual-purpose crewbus with five seats and a rear loadspace for mail. LDV Pilots delivered to this specification up to 2002 were coded 78. The 2003 delivery was substantial, 3910001-468, followed by an order for one hundred and forty-six in 2004 with over two hundred delivered by late 2005. This is the only type of LDV Pilot now ordered by Royal Mail. 3910331 is used as a postbus at Aberfeldy in Scotland, while 5910134 was tried at Penrith, but its five seats were insufficient for the afternoon postbus services.

Types 92 to 95

Type code 92 has been used just once, in 1985, for a batch of six hundred diesel-engined Ford Fiesta mailcars. These were the final purchase of mailcars following the 1983 experiments with Ford Fiestas and Ford Escorts (type codes 00 and 11). No further mailcars were bought and they

The Mailvan Handbook

Newly resprayed Ford Fiesta mailcar C428OBB (5920021) at Otterburn PO in May 1990 *P Eckersley*

An extensive trial of lpg powered vehicles at Mount Pleasant in central London and at Perth commenced in 2003, using one hundred and forty-eight lpg powered vehicles comprising: seventy-nine Combos; ten Peugeot Grant crewbuses; two Ford Transit vans; twenty-one Ford Transit six-seat multi-purpose crewbuses and thirty-six LDV Convoy six-seat multi-purpose crewbuses. Illustrated is the first of the twenty-one Ford Transit crewbuses, LG53PXD (2952001) at Ludgate Hill in May 2005. *D Longbottom*

Royal Mail has bought LDV Pilots and its predecessors, the 200 and the Sherpa, virtually every year since 1975 but the only vehicles currently being supplied are 5-seat crewbuses with a rear mail compartment for dual-purpose use as both crewbuses and mailvans. Illustrating one of the current delivery is BU05KCO (5910168) which, despite its Scottish livery, is understood to be operating at Chipping Norton in Oxfordshire. It was photographed at the LDV despatch yard in July 2005 at Washwood Heath awaiting delivery. *C M Hogan*

were replaced with standard mailvans at the end of their service with the Post Office. Fiesta 5920351 was used as a postbus.

The current use of code 92 is on the LDV Convoy high-roof multi-purpose crewbus with six seats. Again this type was coded 78 and the 2003 delivery was numbered 3920001-397, followed by 4920001-31 in 2004 and 5920001 upwards in 2005.

The first use of type code 93 was on fifty 2250cf twin-axle box semi-trailers taken on lease from TiP for three years for parcels work. Later the code was used in 1991 for two Renault Extra 80cf vans taken in the fleet after demonstration work.

The use of type code 94 is similar in that it was used in 1986 for two skeletal semi-trailers on lease from TiP, and in 1991 for two Renault Trafic vans bought after evaluation as 150cf mailvans.

Type code 95 was used in 1986 for 239 12.2m 2250cf semi-trailers on lease from TiP for three years for parcels work, these are thought to have differed from those coded 93 in having roller-bed internal floors and in 1991 for two Renault Master vans bought after evaluation as 400cf mailvans. Code 95 was reused again in 2002 with a small batch of Ford Transit 6-seat multi-purpose crewbuses with lpg/petrol engines numbered 2952001-21. They have the same layout as the standard LDV Convoy coded 92.

The Mailvan Handbook

Types 96 to 99

Type code 96 was allocated in 1986 to seventy-four Crane-Fruehauf 10/11m box semi-trailers taken on lease from TiP for parcels work. It was used again in 2003 for a batch of LDV Convoy petrol/lpg 6-seat multi-purpose crewbuses, 3960001-36, as part of the trial in central London of lpg propulsion. Apart from their fuel, they are identical to standard type code 92 crewbuses.

Type code 97 is used for various miscellaneous pieces of equipment, such as gritter trailers and mobile conveyor belts. Type code 98 was allocated in 1982 to a Dodge 50-series mobile X-ray van.

Finally, type code 99 was allocated in 1971 to vehicles, mainly cars, used by Girobank. After the sale of Girobank to the Alliance & Leicester Building Society in July 1990, the code has remained unused.

The Royal Mail Group has a Management and Conference Centre at Coton House on the outskirts of Rugby. Minibuses are used to bring delegates to the centre from Rugby rail station and a replacement was required for blue LDV Convoy 16-seat minibus P928GOM (6780401). Mercedes-Benz Vario O814 with Frank Guy 22-seat bodywork and Ratcliff wheelchair lift at the rear BV04AFA (3755001) was delivered in August 2004 but was found to be unsuitable for its intended use at Coton House, and a standard LDV Convoy postbus was used instead. The Mercedes is pictured in September 2004 at Coventry workshop. It was auctioned and is now operated by Blue Line of Maghull on Merseyside. *C M Hogan*

British Postal Museum and Archive

Royal Mail Group donated the collection of the former National Postal Museum to the British Postal Museum & Archive (BPMA) in 2004. The former National Postal Museum had relatively small galleries, and it could only ever display a small portion of the collection. The collection is as diverse as the activities of the Post Office and Royal Mail. It ranges from the small, such as handstamps, labels and telephone headsets, to the very large, such as Mobile Post Office vehicles and the Travelling Post Office coach. The collection is constantly being developed to reflect the rôle of people in the postal service, and the innovations in technology to meet the demands of a changing world. They are housed at a store at Debden in Essex, and the BPMA has open days to its collection each summer. For more information: www.postalheritage.org.uk/collections.

The oldest vehicle in the collection is a pre-war Morris Minor 35cf mailvan, BXW507 (0240) from May 1935, followed by the later hybrid version in the form of 1938 Minor EXM448. The collection includes examples of a 1946 Morris-Commercial LCS 240cf mailvan, a 1951 Morris series Z mailvan, a 1956 Morris-Commercial LC5 mailvan and a 1957 Morris-Commercial KNC mailvan. Many of the principal designs purchased in the 1960s and 1970s are featured in collection, as well as two Post Office Telephones vehicles, a 1946 Morris-Commercial CV11/40 and a 1956 Morris JB.

The Morris Minor was the standard small mailvan between 1953 and 1971. One of the vehicles in the British Postal Museum and Archive's collection is this October 1961 van, 194CXN (71053), which operated for Head Postmaster Shrewsbury until March 1967. *C M Hogan*

The Morris, later Austin-Morris, J4 was bought between 1961 and 1974 by the GPO and the Post Office. PGF256L (2050233) is from the 1972 delivery and was allocated to Sutton, Surrey but on replacement, it was retained as a workshop runabout at Banstead for many years. It was restored to near original condition at Kidbrooke repair depot in south-east London. *M W Skillen*

The appearance of a model of a Royal Mail Reliant Supervan mailvan in the Vanguard range of models caused much comment as collectors had forgotten the purchase of a batch of fifty of these vans by the Post Office in 1970. They had a very short life as mailvans and none survived for preservation but the Post Office purchased a contemporary blue car, converted it to a van and finished it in Royal Mail livery. It was photographed in September 1995 at a Royal Mail Funday at Duxford shortly after conversion. It is now part of the BPMA's vehicle collection. *C M Hogan*

The last mailvan bought with traditional coachbuilt bodywork was the Morris 420LD 360cf bodywork. Retained from the final batch delivered in 1970-71 is LYM228K (275906) with SCWS bodywork that was allocated to the Inland Section at Mount Pleasant in London. It was photographed shortly after restoration in 1992. *C M Hogan*

The collection includes both the 1957 Seddon motive unit GPO 2 and the 1937 Mobile Post Office semi-trailer with Duple bodywork on a Brockhouse chassis, as well as the later 1971 Karrier Gamecock tender and trailer GGO926J (1820001). The Seddon and its semi-trailer have recently been thoroughly restored and renovated at Cartwrights in Altrincham.

One of the Trust's main aims is to allow public access – physical, virtual and by out-reach - to the collections and archives. Key to the Trust's future therefore is the establishment of a permanent home for the collection now stored at Debden and the Archive at Freeling House. The vehicles and larger artefacts have never been on public display apart from the short period when the former public counter area at King Edward Building housed a few small vehicles, and Debden is little more than a warehouse. The conservation and preservation work on the current collection continues and as the fleet is ever-changing, so, selected current models need to be set aside as they come to the end of their careers. Plans are advancing for various events in 2006 to mark the centenary of the first motor vehicle to be owned by the GPO. Apart from open days at Debden there are plans to hold events at various museums, including Gaydon, Beaulieu, Leyland and Sunderland, together with a static exhibition in Scotland.

ISBN 1 904875 03 3

© Published by *British Bus Publishing Ltd, December 2005*.

British Bus Publishing Ltd, 16 St Margaret's Drive, Telford, TF1 3PH
Telephone: 01952 255669 - Facsimile: 01952 222397

www.britishbuspublishing.co.uk - E-mail sales@britishbuspublishing.co.uk